A
GOURMET'S
GUIDE TO

FRUIT

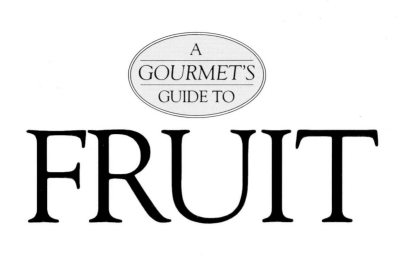

FRUIT

A GOURMET'S GUIDE TO

JUDY BASTYRA
&
JULIA CANNING

Photography by
DAVID JOHNSON

HPBooks ·
a division of
PRICE STERN SLOAN
Los Angeles

HPBooks
A division of Price Stern Sloan, Inc.
360 North La Cienega Boulevard
Los Angeles, California 90048

9 8 7 6 5 4 3 2 1

This book was created by Merehurst Limited
Ferry House, 51/57 Lacy Road, London SW15 1PR

Commissioned and Directed by Merehurst Limited
Photography: David Johnson
Food Stylist: Maria Kelly
Home Economists: Maxine Clark & Lyn Rutherford
Color reproduction by Kentscan, England
Printed in Belgium by Proost International Book Production, Turnhout

Library of Congress Cataloging-in-Publication Data

Bastrya, Judy.
  A gourmet's guide to fruits / by Judy Bastrya & Julia Canning.
    p.   cm.
  ISBN 0-89586-849-0
  1. Cookery (Fruit)   2. Fruit.   I. Canning. Julia.   II. Title.
TX811.B38   1990
641.3'4—dc20   89-15592
                                                                        CIP

Contents

Introduction

The fruits of the earth have never been available to us in so much variety and abundance. From the exotic lychee to the ubiquitous apple, there is sure to be something to delight the eye and palate throughout the year, wherever you are.

But although the increasing appearance of more unusual fruits in our shops has aroused our curiosity and appetite, few of us know what to look for when making a purchase or what to do with these fruits when we get them home. This book aims to take the mystique out of the mangosteen and other esoteric delights, as well as providing you with fresh information and ideas on how to prepare, serve and cook more popular produce.

Each fruit is described in clear, precise detail with superb color photographs for ease of identification. The text provides a general description of each fruit, with details of origin and varieties available, as well as a useful guide to buying, choosing and storing. The imaginative selection of recipes which follows uses a wide range of fruits in dishes for every course—from soups to cocktails!

We hope this book will inspire you to experiment with new and exotic fruits and show you how to use more familiar fruits in a fresh and imaginative way.

Apple

Discovery

The apple *(Malus sylvestris)* is the most widely cultivated fruit in temperate regions. Apple trees will grow easily in most countries in the right conditions, provided they get a cold resting period in winter and are not hampered by frost during flowering.

Apples are especially valued for their storing qualities and until the 20th century they were practically the only fresh fruit available during the winter in cold climates.

There are well over 3,000 varieties of apple cultivated today, a number which is decreasing with the development of high yielding varieties for commerce which guarantee a uniformity of size and color.

Apples can be divided in two basic categories, eating and cooking. Most eating apples are roughly the same size—between 3 to 4 inches in diameter—with smooth or slightly rough skins. They vary in color from green, to yellow with mottled red, to red. The quality of the pulp may be soft and mealy or crisp and hard.

They generally taste sweet, although some can be quite acidic. All should have a juicy bite. Many varieties are good for cooking as well as eating.

Cooking apples tend to be larger than dessert apples. They usually have a smooth skin which is often green but can also be yellow to red. They are juicy and acidic with a tart taste, and while some varieties can be eaten raw, as a rule they need to be sweetened with sugar and cooked. Their distinguishing culinary characteristic is that they cook down to a puree.

EATING APPLES

Cox's Orange Pippin: This fine apple was developed from seed by Richard Cox in about 1825. The pulp is crisp, sweet, and juicy with an acidic bent. It has a mottled yellow and red color and makes an excellent partner with cheese.

Golden Delicious: This has a thin skin with a crispy, light, juicy pulp,

Starking

Golden Delicious

Cox's Orange Pippin

Granny Smith

but can be lacking in flavor. It varies in color from green to yellow, depending on its ripeness. When it turns yellow the apple is much sweeter but less firm.

Granny Smith: This apple is usually bright green, though sometimes flushed with brown or orange. Its pulp is sweet, acidic and juicy. This popular apple tastes good raw, in salads and apple tarts.

Starking: A French variety with a red streaky skin and sweet juicy white pulp.

Worcester Pearmain: A thick pale-green to yellow skin, with heavy crimson markings. The pulp is white, sweet and slightly tough.

Egremont Russet: A sturdy rough skinned apple with a firm, crisp, slightly musty-tasting pulp.

McIntosh: This American apple has a smooth skin with deep red flecks. Its pulp is slightly tart and is good for cooking as well as eating.

Spartan: A red-skinned apple flushed with yellow, originally from Denmark. Its pulp has a custard-like flavor.

Red Delicious: A very popular American variety with a bright red skin and a firm, sweet, juicy pulp.

Laxton's Superb: A popular English apple with a yellow and red mottled skin and a crisp juicy flavor.

Other apple varieties available are **Pippin, Jonathan, Rome** and **Gala.**

COOKING APPLES
Bramley's Seedling, Grenadier and **Newton Wonder** are fairly similar in appearance with Bramley's Seedling being the most popular of the English cooking varieties. A large apple with a rather waxy, thin green skin, sometimes flushed with red. It has a tart, acidic flavor and is excellent for use as a cooking apple.

Choosing & Storing
When choosing apples, look for those with tight smooth unblemished skins. Avoid any that look bruised and remove them if they become so once you get them home, to avoid contaminating their neighbors. A general rule is that bright red apples tend to have slightly mealy pulp and bright green apples are often immature and lacking in flavor. You can generally tell a ripe apple by the fullness of its aroma. Immature apples will ripen at

Bramley's Seedling

Spartan

Royal Gala

Worcester Pearmain

Red Delicious

Laxton's Superb

home although there are exceptions to this rule. It is always good to ask the supplier's advice.

If you have fruit from the garden or have been apple picking, you can store the fruit as follows: wrap them individually in newspaper or small unsealed plastic bags, then pack on slatted racks or wooden boxes. Wrapping them will prevent any spoilage spreading from one apple to another. Store in an airy room or a cool, frost-free place, such as a cellar or shed.

If you prefer to store prepared apples, apple puree freezes well; raw apple slices mixed with sugar in the ratio of one-half cup of sugar to one pound of fruit, and raw apple slices packed in a sugar syrup also freeze successfully. All will keep well for approximately six months. To use, thaw at room temperature for three to four hours and then use as quickly as possible to prevent discoloration.

Preparation & Cooking
One of the most important things to remember when preparing apples is that they turn brown when cut. To prevent discoloration, put them in lightly salted or acidulated water as you peel or cut them. Alternatively toss them in lemon or lime juice.

Always core apples before you peel them if you want to keep them whole; they tend to collapse if they are cored after they have been peeled. An attractive way of presenting apples is to quarter, core and slice them in sections, or core them and cut in rings.

Apples have always been associated with pork; they are also excellent served with game. In France, the Normandy region specializes in cooking dishes—both sweet and savory—with apples. Eating apples are excellent in salads, such as the famous Waldorf salad—a combination of apples, celery, walnuts and mayonnaise.

They can also be cooked as fritters, Chinese toffee apples (apples coated in toffee and sesame seeds), stewed, and in flans and tarts, such as the delicious *Tarte Tatin* from France. They may be coated with toffee or caramel or a recent variation on this, chocolate-and-nut covered.

Cooking apples are excellent baked, or pureed with lemon juice. Like eating apples, their flavor is enhanced by the addition of spices, such as cinnamon and cloves. They may be stuffed and baked, fried as an accompaniment to meat and, of course, what can beat a hot apple pie with ice cream as a favorite family treat.

Pureed apple is used to make a traditional sauce to accompany meat and poultry. It is also used to make apple butter, which was introduced to America by the Dutch many years ago, and has since become a popular spread.

There are many by-products from apples, including apple juice and cider—which is made from varieties of apple with a high tannin content. From cider a distilled liquor called applejack is made. In France it is called apple brandy or Calvados. Cider vinegar of course is also produced from cider. Pectin, used for setting jams and jellies, is extracted from the skins and cores of apples. Dried apple rings are popular in compotes and muesli-type cereals, as well as being a useful method of preserving the fruit.

Crab Apple

The crab apple *(Malus pumila)* is the parent species of the modern cultivated apple. It grows wild all over Europe, America and Asia; it is also planted in gardens for its decorative appearance. The fruit is similar to a cherry, though slightly larger and sometimes elongated as well as round. The crab apple has a sharp astringent taste and is suitable only for cooking. It is used to make delicious jams and jellies. Indeed, crab apple jelly is an excellent alternative to red currant jelly, as an accompaniment to roast lamb.

Pear

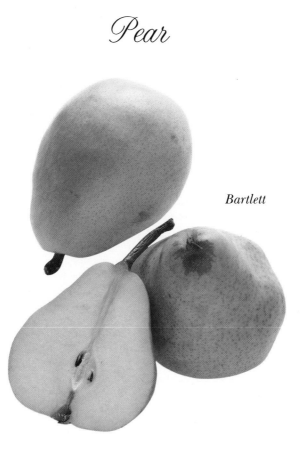

Bartlett

Packham

Most of the pears available today are descended from the common pear *(Pyrus communis)*. Native to the Middle East and Eastern Europe, the pear tree thrives in warm conditions and ideally like a rich, moist soil. Pear trees need a warmer environment than apple trees. By the 17th century, France had become the most important country for pear cultivation and, from the 1700s onwards, French and Belgian gardeners were chiefly responsible for the fine varieties that are grown today. However two of the most popular varieties, Bartlett and Conference pears, were raised by British gardeners in Berkshire.

The major pear producers these days include France, Belgium, Britain, Holland, West Germany, Spain, Australia, South Africa and the United States.

Like apples, pears are generally divided into eating (dessert) and cooking types, although many dessert pears are also used for cooking. The characteristic gritty texture of the pear pulp has been bred out of many of the better dessert types, but is still very noticeable in the cooking varieties. Dessert pears are also much juicier and sweeter than the cooking type.

Bartlett: In England this variety is called Williams' Bon Chrétien, named after the person who first distributed the fruit in Britain. The Bartlett has a pale green to golden yellow skin, which is patched or dotted with russet, and sometimes tinged with red. Roundish in shape, it has a creamy white pulp which is soft, juicy and deliciously flavored. The ripe fruit is best eaten raw, but when slightly immature may be used for cooking.

Doyenné du Comice: A large, oval-shaped fruit with a pale yellow skin, which has occasional russet fiecks. The juicy pulp is creamy white with a melting texture and has a sweet, aromatic flavor, making it perfect for eating raw.

Conference: This pear was named after the 1885 National British Pear Conference where it was exhibited. The Conference is long in shape and the skin is dark green with russet patches. Firm and juicy, with sweet-flavored creamy-pink pulp, the Conference is good for cooking as well as for eating raw.

Beurré Hardy: This pear has a roughish yellow-green skin, patched with russet. The ripe fruit, which has slightly pink, sweet pulp, is delicious eaten raw, but the underripe fruit is good for cooking.

Packham and **Beurré d'Amanlis** are two other common varieties. A popular cooking pear is the **Passacrassana** which has a tough, gritty skin but a good flavor pulp.

Bosc and **d'Anjou** are winter pears, excellent for both cooking and eating.

Asian Pear: A large, round fruit, with a pale yellow skin and firm, scented pulp. Similar in many ways to the common pear, the Asian pear is becoming increasingly available.

Buying & Storing
Once pears ripen, they deteriorate very quickly, so it is probably best to buy the fruit when it is still slightly firm and allow it to ripen at home in a warm, dark place. A ripe pear will give a little when pressed gently at the neck. Ripe pears should be eaten within a day; if refrigerated, they will last for a few days, if necessary.

Freezing is a good long term way of storing pears. Poach halved pears in a sugar syrup, then freeze for up to eight months.

Preparation & Cooking
A ripe, juicy pear at its peak, is a delight to serve alone as a fresh dessert fruit, while its scented pulp also makes it an interesting addition to many sweet and savory dishes. The pulp is extremely fragile, so handle with care at all times.

To prepare pear halves, simply scoop out the soft cores with a teaspoon, then brush with lemon juice to prevent discoloration. To prepare a whole pear, remove the core by working an apple corer in from the bottom.

Cheese and pears have now become a popular combination, and a refreshing way to end a meal is to serve fresh pears with Brie, Camembert or Stilton. Pear halves filled with a Roquefort cheese dressing, and shellfish coated in a herb-flavored mayonnaise, make excellent starters.

The fresh, sweet flavor of pears adds an unusual touch to watercress or fresh spinach salads, particularly when dressed with a lemon-based vinaigrette. Sliced pears make an attractive topping to tarts and a fragrant filling for savory flans—particularly good when partnered with tarragon and ricotta cheese.

Poaching whole pears in syrup is perhaps the best known way of cooking the fruit. This gentle method of cooking preserves the shape of the delicate pulp and adds flavor. Pears poached in red wine, flavored with cinnamon, is a classic, but the fruit is equally delicious poached in syrups flavored with vanilla, ginger, lemon or orange juice, or other fruit such as raspberries and currants. Chopped nuts are ideal toppings.

Poires à l'Impératrice is traditionally made by topping a creamy rice mold with poached pears, while *Poires Belle-Hélène* is a creation of poached pears, arranged on vanilla ice cream and served with chocolate sauce.

Pear soufflés, sorbets and jams are delicious and you can use dessert pears to make sweet chutneys, and cooking pears to make pickles, spiced with cloves and nutmeg. The pear *eau-de-vie*, which is known as Poire William, is useful for flavoring desserts. Very often the liqueur has a whole pear inside the bottle.

Beurré Hardy

Asian Pear

Conference

Doyenné du Comice

Quince

Quince

The common quince *(Cydonia oblonga or Cydonia vulgaris)* resembles a pear or an apple in shape, according to variety. The skin is golden when ripe and the pulp, which is firm and inedible when raw, is quite aromatic.

Probably originating in Iran, quinces are grown today in Turkey, South America and all over the Mediterranean.

The Japanese quince, or **japonica,** now classed as *Chaenomeles* is related to the common quince. It produces fruit with a slightly more acidic flavor which can be used for jams and jellies.

Buying & Storing
Select firm fruit which is unblemished. Store in a cool, dry place, well spaced and apart from other food, as the fruit has a strong, penetrating aroma. Quinces that have been poached in a light sugar syrup can be frozen for up to six months.

Preparation & Cooking
The sharp, hard pulp of quince softens on cooking and turns an attractive pink color. To prepare fruit, remove skin and core, then put into water acidulated with lemon juice to prevent discoloration.

The pungent flavor of quince is a good foil to rich meat, and in Middle Eastern cookery the quince is stewed with lamb and game or stuffed with meat mixed with spiced lentils. The Moroccan *tajine* often combines lamb or chicken with quince. A quince sauce makes an excellent substitute for applesauce to serve with roast pork.

Quinces are commonly made into jams and jellies because of their high pectin content. In France, Spain and the Middle East, the fruit is turned into a confection, which is called *cotignac* in France. This is a thick paste, made by boiling down the fruit to a puree with sugar; the paste is cut in pieces and served as a confection or, in the Spanish tradition, with cheese. Quinces also make a good addition to apple and pear pies and the puree makes a delicately scented fruit fool.

Medlar

The strangely shaped medlar *(Mespilus germanica)* looks rather like a small russet-brown apple, but has an extraordinary calyx in the middle, surrounding a depression which holds five visible seed vessels.

Probably native to southeast Europe and central Asia, the medlar is hardier than the quince and now grows wild throughout Europe. The ripe fruit is hard and inedible and has to be kept until it has been allowed to turn brown and soft, almost rotted. Medlars are fairly rare these days, though some people still regard them as a great delicacy. The Victorians were very fond of medlars and served them with port. Today they are mainly used for making a fragrant jelly.

Cherry

Sweet Cherries (hybrid varieties)

Closely related to the plum, the cherry is a small, round, pitted fruit, ranging in color from purple-black to yellow-orange. There are basically two important types—sweet cherries *(Prunus avium)* and sour cherries *(Prunus cerasus)*. There are also hybrids between the sweet and sour cherries which are generally known as **Dukes**.

The Romans first introduced cherries to western Europe and some varieties are almost unchanged since then. Today cherries are grown in most temperate climates, in Europe and the United States in particular.

SWEET CHERRIES

These are mainly intended for eating as a dessert fruit. The pulp is usually sweet but sometimes verges on the bitter side. Popular varieties include **Early Rivers** which are large, dark-crimson and deliciously sweet, and **Bigarreau Napoleons,** which are pale yellow, tinged with red, and have firm pulp. **Lambert** and **Bing** are favorite American varieties. Both are dark-red and have a good flavor.

SOUR CHERRIES

These are particularly good for cooking and are usually sold as **Morello** cherries. Highly acidic, Morellos are dark-red in color and very juicy. Lighter-colored sour cherries are sold as **amarelles**.

The hybrid **Dukes** can be black or red and their characterful flavor makes them ideal for cooking. They are sometimes called Royales.

Buying & Storing

Look for shiny, plump, unblemished fruit. Avoid cherries that are split, as this is a sign of over-ripeness. Sweet cherries should have their stalks attached.

Ripe cherries are highly perishable and ideally should be eaten on the day of purchase. However, if loosely wrapped, they will keep for up to two days in the refrigerator. Cherries can be frozen.

Preparation & Cooking

Sweet cherries served fresh as a dessert fruit are a true summer treat. To pit cherries, press out the pits with a cherry pitter, or push pit through with a skewer.

Sweet cherries are not usually used for cooking, but they do make a colorful addition to fruit salads. Mixed with sweetened whipped cream, they are a delicious filling for crepes, cakes and pastries.

The fresh taste of sour cherries goes well in dishes made with rich meat, such as duck, and the flavor marries perfectly with almonds.

A popular cherry recipe is the luscious Black Forest Gateau; from France comes the classic batter and cherry dessert, Clafoutis. American cherry pie is irresistible served with cream, while the elegant, flamed Cherries Jubilee is traditionally served with ice cream. Cherries also make wonderful jams and ices.

The liqueurs made from cherries are invaluable for flavoring dishes—particularly kirsch. Maraschino is a much sweeter liqueur.

Peach

The downy, velvety skin of the peach *(Prunus persica)* encloses a firm, but delectably juicy pulp. The skin can vary in color from pale cream flushed with red to golden yellow with a crimson blush that can almost cover the entire fruit. In the center of the fruit is a large crinkly pit.

Peaches originally came from China but eventually reached Europe, probably via Persia, and are now grown in most warm climates. Countries where they are grown include the United States, France, Italy, Spain, Greece, Australia and South Africa. Fruit for export is picked while still firm and ripened at room temperature. However, the taste can suffer.

There are hundreds of different varieties of peach, but they all have either yellow or white pulp. Sometimes they are grouped and described as either clingstones, when the pulp adheres to the pit, or freestones, when the pulp comes away from the pit easily.

Buying & Storing

Choose fruit that is still firm but without a hint of green—look for a yellow or cream tinge beneath the blush. Avoid fruit that is too soft as it is not as tasty.

Ripe peaches will keep in the refrigerator for about a week. Peaches freeze well when poached in sugar syrup.

Preparation & Cooking

A perfectly, ripe sweet peach, eaten on its own, is an exquisite experience, but peaches are also used in a variety of dishes.

To peel peaches, dip them in boiling water for 15 to 20 seconds, depending on ripeness, then plunge into cold water. To pit a peach, cut in half around the pit, then twist apart. Rub exposed pulp with lemon juice to prevent discoloration. If serving uncooked, prepare within an hour of serving.

A classically simple way to serve ripe peach halves is to sprinkle them with a little superfine sugar, then top with white wine or medium-dry sherry. An excellent way of treating slightly underripe peaches is to make a compote: poach lightly in a sugar syrup before adding liqueur. Peaches poached in this manner can be used to make Peach Melba—peach halves topped with ice cream, raspberry puree and nuts.

Grilled peaches are good with ice cream, and peach slices make a decorative topping to tarts. The delicate flavor goes well with duck, and pickled peaches complement cold meats.

Nectarine

The nectarine is a smooth-skinned variety of the peach with a richer flavor and a skin which is quite pleasant to eat.

When buying nectarines, look for firmish fruit, with no hint of green in the shiny skins. Prepare and serve as for peaches.

Apricot

Looking rather like a small peach, the skin of the apricot *(Prunus armeniaca)* varies in color from pale yellow to deep orange; some have a natural freckling, others a pink blush. The firm pulp, which is white to orange in color, has a sharper flavor than the peach, making it ideal for savory and sweet dishes.

Apricots probably originated in Asia and gradually worked their way across Europe to arrive in England during the 16th century. Later, the apricot was introduced to America where, in California, it is now grown in large quantities. Other important growers include Afghanistan, Iran, Spain, Greece, China and North Africa.

A warm, ripe apricot picked off the tree is sheer delight but, like the peach, it is unfortunately often

Nectarine

Peach

Apricot

picked slightly unripe for export—and the flavor is impaired.

Buying & Storing
Select unblemished fruit with velvety skins. If necessary, store ripe apricots for up to two days in the bottom of the refrigerator. They also freeze well in a sugar syrup.

Preparation & Cooking
Apricots are delicious eaten raw, and are best served at room temperature. The fruit is also valued for its culinary versatility.

To peel apricots, immerse them in boiling water for one minute, then peel. To pit the fruit, simple cut in half and twist apart.

Apricots have always been a great favorite in patisserie—halved apricots make delectable tarts, and apricot glaze is used endlessly.

Apricots may be served as a compote, or the cooked fruit pureed and used in fruit foods, ice creams, sorbets, soufflés or sauces.

In the Middle East, apricots are a popular ingredient with lamb. They also combine well with duck or chicken—try adding chopped apricots to a poultry stuffing.

Plum

Royson

The plum *(Prunus domestica)* is a hybrid of the cherry plum and the sloe. The greengage, damson and mirabelle are also treated as part of the cultivated plum family, although they are often categorized separately. Plums will grow fairly easily in the right conditions—usually a cold winter and a warm summer—in most warm temperate climates. Varieties grown in America are the direct descendants of the Japanese Plum (which is in fact from China), while the British varieties come originally from western Asia. Plums are available throughout the year, being exported from Spain, Germany, North and South America, the Balkans, North Africa and South Africa.

Plums can be roughly divided into three categories: cooking, dessert or eating and wild plums. The fruits vary enormously in color, size, taste and shape. The skin can be red, yellow, purple or orange, while the pulp varies from green to yellow, purple or red. There are those whose pit is closely attached—clingstone—and others whose pit is quite loose—freestone. Over 1,000 named varieties of plum exist in Europe while quite a few are indigenous to America—California grows over forty species alone. Most of them (apart from the wild varieties) may be eaten raw and nearly all are excellent cooked.

DESSERT PLUMS

Dessert plums tend to be juiciest, with a higher sugar content and a better flavor than cooking plums.

Victoria: Perhaps one of the best known varieties of plum in Britain. It is a heavy cropping plum, oval in shape, with a yellow skin heavily flushed with red. The pulp is sweet and juicy with a rather bland flavor. A great favorite for canning, compotes and pies.

Japanese Plum: This ranges in color from yellow to orange through to red and has a rather bland flavor.

Red Beauty: A juicy plum, dark-red when ripe, with a lighter-red pulp.

Royson: An American variety with a bright red, yellow-speckled skin.

Santa Rosa: Perhaps the most famous of the American dessert plums, it is large and round with a dark-red skin. The pulp is juicy and sweet, with a perfumed taste.

Gages: Thought originally to have come from Asia Minor, the most famous of this old variety of plum is the greengage. Introduced to England in 1724 by Sir William Gage from France, where it is called *reineclaude*, the greengage is green, small and round. It has a sweet, juicy, almost translucent pulp, which has a delicate aromatic flavor. It is perhaps the finest of all the eating plums. The French greengage tends to be larger and better flavored than the British. It is perfect served as a dessert fruit after a meal or it can be made into delicious jams, pies and tarts.

Red Beauty

Japanese

Santa Rosa

Mirabelle: Another delicately flavored fruit, smaller than the other plums. It is yellow, often flushed with red, and has a firm sweet pulp. It is grown primarily in Alsace and is also excellent for preserves. The Mirabelle plum is well known for its *eau-de-vie* (brandy).

COOKING PLUMS

Cooking plums have rather acidic, dry pulp. Like the dessert plums, they vary in color from blueish-black (the majority) to greenish-yellow or purplish-red. They also vary in shape.

Pershore Egg: The best known of the British cooking varieties, although it may also be eaten raw. It has a yellow or red-tinted skin and is mostly used for making jam.

Laxton's Cropper: One of many English Laxton plus, the Cropper is a versatile cooking plum.

Stanley: Originally from America, this is a popular cooking plum.

Quetsch: Perhaps the best known cooking plum in eastern Europe, this small, dark fruit is used for making dumplings, tarts and *eau-de-vie* (brandy).

Damson: The plum from Damascus, as it was called by the crusaders, is more elongated than other plums with a pointed end. It has a rich blueish-purple color when ripe, and a strong tart flavor. The damson is excellent for jams, pies, dumplings and purees. This strong-flavored plum is also used to make wine and a flavored gin.

WILD PLUMS

Wild plums can be found in many countries in the northern hemisphere, from the Pacific Coast of America to Japan.

Bullace: Small, round, blue-black plum, with an acidic flavor. Good for preserves.

Sloe: Also known as the blackthorn, this small round black fruit has green, acidic, inedible pulp, which is only used to make sloe gin and sloe wine.

Buying & Storing

When choosing either dessert or cooking plums, avoid any that are bruised or damaged or too soft. Dessert plums should be ripe but firm, with a bloom on the skin. It is always better to buy them a little on the underripe side as they will ripen at home within a few days. Ripe plums should be eaten as soon as possible. Plums freeze well.

Preparation & Cooking

Many people find the skin of plums difficult to digest. For purees, remove the skin as you would for a tomato, by blanching in boiling water. If you want the plums to keep their shape, do not remove skins; halve, pit and poach them in water, adding sugar afterwards.

Cooking plums are delightful in compotes on their own, or combined with other summer fruits. They may be pureed, made into sauces—sweet and savory—and served with duck, pork and goose, or made into ice creams, sorbets, jams, chutneys, pies and flans.

Loquat

Similar in shape and size to a plum, the loquat (*Eriobotrya japonica*) has juicy, cream-colored, slightly tart pulp. The golden skin is thin and downy and there are large shiny pits in the center of the fruit.

Often referred to as Japanese Medlar, the loquat is in fact native to both China and Japan. It was first introduced into the Mediterranean region by the French and is now also grown in the United States, Australia, India and Africa.

Ripe fruit must be eaten at once. Loquats can be served raw—just cut open and remove the pits and their papery skins. They are also delicious poached in a light syrup, flavored with lemon or lime peel and juice. The skins are easier to remove after cooking. Loquat jam is another common use. In Chinese cuisine loquats are cooked with poultry and their flavor enhanced with ginger.

Victoria

Laxton's Cropper

Damson

Stanley

Loquat

Banana

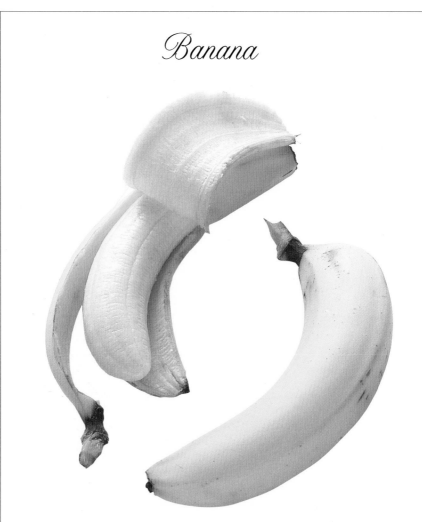

Dessert Bananas

The banana *(Musa sapientum)* is one of the most widely cultivated fruits in the world.

The fruit's origin is usually attributed to India and southern Asia. Today bananas can be found throughout the tropics and subtropics. The main banana-producing areas of the world for export are the West Indies, Central and South America and West Africa. The rarer varieties are exported from Southeast Asia, Australia, New Zealand, South Africa and the Pacific islands. Surprisingly, Iceland is the only European country to grow bananas commercially.

Bananas for export are cut when still green and transported in specially refrigerated ships. The temperature is kept between 53F to 55F (12C to 13C). They are then hung to ripen in warmed rooms. They must never be kept at a colder temperature or they will turn black. Bananas are highly nutritious and form the staple food in some parts of the Third World.

There are basically two types of banana, dessert and cooking, both of which are available throughout the year. The dessert or eating banana can be eaten raw and is sweet whereas the cooking banana, also known as plantain, has to be cooked before you can eat it. Dessert bananas that are green and unripe can also be used for cooking.

DESSERT BANANAS
Most eating bananas are usually marketed under a brand name rather than by variety. However, they tend to be of a similar quality and flavor. They are gently curved in a crescent shape and vary in length between 6 to 12 inches. Depending on the ripeness, their skins can be green, yellow or brown, and have a creamy-white, soft pulp—the riper the banana, the sweeter the pulp.

Plantain

Lady's Fingers

Dessert Bananas

Dessert Bananas

Rice Banana: One of the more unusual varieties of eating banana available in the shops today. They are between 1-1/2 to 3 inches long and have a yellow unribbed skin enclosing a rather sweet, easily digestible pulp.

Lady's Fingers: The most popular of the small varieties of dessert bananas, these are bright yellow with a thin skin and a very sweet flavor. The taste is slightly reminiscent of apple.

Red Bananas: As their name suggests, these have a red skin and pink pulp. They are quite plump and vary considerably in size from about five inches to much larger. When ripe, the pulp is very sweet and slightly sticky.

COOKING BANANAS

The plantain, or cooking banana, tends to be much larger and fatter then the dessert banana, and with a thicker skin. The pulp is dense and starchy when unripe, becoming sticky as it ripens. It has a milder flavor than a dessert banana, which becomes stronger with maturity.

Buying & Storing

When choosing bananas, make sure the skin is unbroken and there are no large brown patches. Otherwise, selecting bananas is really a matter of personal choice. As a general guide, yellow dessert bananas are fully ripe and sweet when the skins have a few brown speckles. Red bananas will give slightly when gently pressed. Cooking bananas or plantain can be cooked when totally unripe and green as a starch vegetable in a stew, or as they ripen when they turn yellow then brown, almost black. Always store bananas and plantains at room temperature; never refrigerate or freeze or they will turn black.

Preparation & Cooking

Bananas are best prepared just before serving. Once they are peeled, toss them in lemon or lime juice to prevent them turning brown.

Unripe cooking bananas or plantains are difficult to peel. Cut them in half crosswise, then score along the ridges and pare off the skin sections. They tend to stain your hands, so peel under running cold water.

Ripe plantains peel easily as eating bananas. Like bananas, they can also be cooked in their skins—boiled, baked or grilled. In India these bananas are often curried in their skins.

Dessert bananas are most often associated with sweet dishes: trifles, ice creams, fruit salads and milk shakes. They can also be made into bread and cakes and delicious alcoholic cocktails.

Cooking bananas or plantains feature a great deal in Caribbean, African and Indian cooking. When unripe they are cut up and cooked as a staple ingredient in soups and stews. They may also be fried, boiled and curried.

Another popular way of preparing plantains in the Caribbean is to cover them with lots of onions and lime juice after they have been boiled.

Once ripe, plantains can also be thinly sliced and deep-fried like chips—delicious and they will keep for quite a while if stored in an airtight container.

Bananas may be dried in the same way as pears or apricots, or by a different method which produces crisp chips for cereal and dried fruit mixes. A product of dried bananas is banana flour which is very easily digested. Some varieties of banana are also used to make beer.

It is not only the fruit of the banana plant that is used in cooking. The heart of the banana flower, before it opens, and the central part of the stem can also be eaten.

Finally, banana leaves are used as both containers for food and for wrapping and flavoring Indian, Mexican, Venezuelan and West Indian dishes, such as *tamales* or *pastelles* (cornmeal and spicy meat bundles). Banana leaves are available in some Chinese and Southeast Asian supermarkets. They are sold already stripped from the central stem and should be passed quickly over a naked flame, to release the smoky-flavored oil and make them more pliable for wrapping.

Fig

Figs

A pear-shaped fruit, the fig *(Ficus carica)* is known for its biblical connections. The fruit contains a soft, juicy red pulp which is full of minute edible seeds. The skin can vary in color from white to black to purple to green. It was once one of the basic foods of the Mediterrean, though its nutritive value is not outstanding.

The fig originated in Asia Minor and was spread throughout Europe by the Romans. Today there are hundreds of varieties, but the **Smyrna** figs are still regarded as the best, although **Brown Turkey** is a favorite. In California the Smyrna was crossed to produce the succulent **Calimyrna.**

California, Turkey, North Africa and the Mediterranean countries are important producers.

Buying & Storing
Figs have a surprisingly thin skin; look for unbruised fruit. They are best to eat when soft to the touch, but are highly perishable and should be consumed as soon as possible.

Preparation & Cooking
Fresh figs need no preparation but should be served slightly above room temperature so that the flavor is enhanced. The shape of the figs is its greatest feature: serve whole or halved, accompanied by cream or nuts, or just with liqueurs. Figs are delicious served with cured meat— ideal as a starter. They can also be poached whole in syrup or stewed as a compote. Dried figs may be eaten whole or chopped, used in baking in the same way as other dried fruits.

Date

Fresh Dates

Dried Dates

Fresh dates *(Pheonix dactylifera)* are a relatively new arrival on the Western market. Grown on tall palms, dates are oblong in shape and hold a single cylindrical stone. They are usually about two inches long and yellow-red to dark brown in color, with a shiny, papery skin. The pulp is moist and quite sweet, tasting rather like honey.

Dates are among the oldest known fruits, with a recorded history stretching back to 3000 BC. The tall palms produce either male or female flowers—one male tree is required to pollinate between 50 to 100 females. They grow in arid conditions and consequently dates have always been an important source of food in Arab countries.

It is most likely that dates originated around the Persian Gulf, and in the past North Africa and India have been the traditional date growers. Iraq has also been an important source of dates, along with Saudi Arabia, Algeria, Iran and Egypt. Today, however, dates are also cultivated in California, Spain and Israel.

Dates may be exported either dried and compressed into solid blocks, suitable for eating or cooking; semi-dry as individual fruits in boxes (sometimes still attached to their stand—or a plastic replica of it); fresh and loose; or dried and ground into flour.

Buying & Storing

Choose dates that are shiny and plump. Fresh dates freeze well so they are usually available throughout the year. They should be refrigerated and used within three days. Do not freeze imported fresh dates, as they usually have been frozen earlier.

Select dried dates that still look plump and avoid any which are shrivelled or covered in a layer of sugar crystals.

Preparation & Cooking

Date skins can easily be removed by cutting off the stalk end and pinching the other end so that the pulp pops out. The pit can be pushed or cut out.

Fresh dates are delicious eaten raw, and they are particularly good stuffed with savory fillings. Cream cheese, mixed with chopped nuts or crumbled bacon, is a popular stuffing. In Arab countries, dates are often stuffed with butter.

A simple custom from the Middle East is to serve chilled dates with yogurt. The Moroccan *tajine* features dates, and their natural sweetness makes them ideal for use in brownies or fiber-rich cookies. Wrapped in bacon, dates make excellent hors d'oeuvres.

Dried dates are used in cooking in the same way as other dried fruits: in cakes, pudding, scones, breads, and as a stuffing for apples. They also taste good mixed with apples in pies and tarts and are used to make compotes, chutneys and sauces. Because they are so sweet, less sugar is required when dates are added to tart fruits, such as rhubarb or apple.

Pomegranate

The pomegranate *(Punica granatum)* is a round fruit, the size of an orange, with a crown-like tuft. The leathery thin skin contains a mass of crisp, edible seeds embedded in juicy, translucent, pink pulp. The seeds are divided in compartments by inedible, yellow membranes.

The pomegranate has been known to man for thousands of years, probably originating in Persia, and is surrounded by religious mystique. Today the pomegranate is cultivated in the tropics and subtropics.

Buying & Storing
Look for fruit with a reddish glow and a firm skin. Pomegranates will keep refrigerated for about a week.

Preparation & Cooking
Pomegranates are usually served fresh—the fruit is cut in half and the pulp scooped out. The seeds are usually sucked of their jelly-like pulp and then discarded.

The juice of the pomegranate is used for cooking, particularly in Middle Eastern cuisine. To extract the juice, place the seeds in a sieve and press the juice through. Pomegranate juice is excellent for flavoring desserts, such as ice creams and water ices, and it makes a refreshing long drink. The Iranians use the juice to add a piquancy to soups and meat dishes, and the classic dish *faisinjan* consists of duck or chicken flavored with walnut and pomegranate juice sauce. The French syrup grenadine is based on pomegranate juice.

The jewel-like raw seeds also make a stunning decoration for desserts and salads.

Pomegranates

Persimmon

The persimmon resembles a large, leathery orange-red tomato and has a similar succulent, slightly tart pulp. There are basically two types of persimmons, the American *(Diospyros virginiana)* and the oriental *(Diospyros kaki)*. The American version, which grew wild in Virginia, was discovered as a valuable food by the early settlers. Nowadays the oriental version is more popular in the United States.

The oriental persimmon, commonly known as **Kaki,** originated in Japan and is an important fruit in both Japan and China. Today the kaki is grown all over the subtropics and the Israelis have developed a fruit called the **Sharon Fruit,** which is particularly popular. Kakis have large seeds embedded in their pulp; the sharon fruit is seedless.

Buying & Storing

Kaki fruit should be very ripe before eating; soft, translucent, almost overripe fruit is the best buy, as it will be less bitter. Avoid fruit with split, blemished skins. Sharon fruit on the other hand can be eaten when firm.

Preparation & Cooking

Soft kakis are delicious served on their own; simply slice off the top and dig in with a spoon.

As a first course, the sharon fruit is excellent since it slices so prettily— arrange with smoked meat and sprinkle with vinaigrette.

Tamarillo

An egg-shaped, red fruit, the tamarillo *(Cyphomandra betacea)* has tart orange pulp with small black seeds. The flavor resembles a tomato and the fruit is often referred to as tree tomato. The skin is inedible.

Originating in South America, tamarillos are now cultivated in Southeast Asia, New Zealand and Kenya on a commercial basis.

Buying & Storing

Ripe tamarillos yield to light pressure and will keep refrigerated for about a week. They freeze well.

Preparation & Cooking

Tamarillos can be treated like tomatoes, eaten raw or cooked in savory dishes. Alternatively they make a good addition to desserts.

To remove the skin, place in boiling water for two minutes, then plunge into cold water to cool and peel.

Very often tamarillos are marinated in their own juice: simply slice, sprinkle with sugar and leave for about two hours until the fruit is soft.

Peeled fruit, cut in chunks, is an excellent addition to fruit or vegetable salads; the flavor combines particularly well with kiwifruit in fruit salads.

Sliced tamarillos make a tasty sandwich ingredient when layered with lettuce, cream cheese and cold meat. Grilled, they pair well with hot meat.

On the sweet side, top ice cream, yogurt, cheesecakes and flans with marinated tamarillos.

Jujube

Jujubes are the fruit of the *Zizyphus* tree. The type known as *ber* is a small oval-shaped fruit with green or orange skin. The pulp, which encases a single white pit, has a texture rather like that of an apple and a sweet-sour flavor. Another important species is the Chinese jujube *(Zizyphus jujuba)*.

Grown throughout tropical Africa and Asia, the jujube is chiefly cultivated in India. The fruit is eaten fresh, but is also candied or preserved in syrup. In Sudan, the jujube is traditionally used to make a kind of gingerbread. The fresh fruit will only keep for two to four days, so eat as soon as possible.

Persimmon

Tamarillo

Mango

Cut the mango along the sides of the pit for perfect slices

It is not so many years ago that few people outside the tropics had ever tasted the exotic pulp of a juicy ripe mango. Today mangoes are relatively commonplace, if still expensive, and are sold at most green grocers and supermarkets throughout the year. This is fortunate, because the mango *(Mangifera indica)* is one of the most delicious of all the tropical fruits.

Mangoes vary a great deal in size and shape, from tiny ones the size of a plum to some the size of a small melon, weighing up to two pounds each. They can be round, oval or kidney-shaped and pointed at one end. The most familiar varieties are about the size of a large avocado.

Mangoes have thin, tough, slightly waxy smooth skins which must be peeled. The skin may be green, yellow orange, red or purple. The juicy orange pulp inside can be quite fibrous depending on the quality of the mango—the better the quality the smoother the pulp. Inferior qualities can be quite disappointing— woody with a turpentine-like flavor. The new varieties being cultivated today are juicy and less fibrous. There is a large flat fibrous pit in the center of the fruit which is rather difficult to remove.

Mango pulp tastes juicy and sweet; its slightly perfumed flavor can best be described as acid-sweet, once sampled usually loved. Many people think mangoes are the best fruit in the world.

Summer Mango

Thai

Julie

Alphonso

Mangoes have been cultivated for 4,000 years and came originally from the Indo-Burmese region. They were farmed in India over 2,000 years ago and a great many Hindu legends are connected with the princely mango. Today they are grown in almost every tropical and subtropical country in the world. The biggest exporter of mangoes is India, though many also come from Central and South America, Africa, the West Indies, Egypt and Israel.

The mango comes from the same family as cashews and pistachios. The evergreen trees have large shiny leaves and can grow up to 100 feet. They are best suited to the tropics or subtropics although they can exist in other climates as long as there is no frost and lots of sun while they are flowering.

There are an enormous number of varieties being cultivated today, but among the most popular is the **Alphonso** which is grown in South Africa, Southeast Asia and Florida. It is kidney-shaped and can range in color from green with a red bloom to yellow with red spots. The bright orange pulp has quite a distinctive exotic taste.

Another favorite variety is the **Summer Mango,** again orange and red-skinned with a similar juicy perfumed orange pulp. A West Indian variety which is coveted by the local people is the **Julie** mango. It is a smaller fruit and ranges in color from green to orange when very ripe. It has a distinctive aroma and tastes very sweet and juicy.

There are many varieties which are used only for cooking. They are often smaller than dessert mangoes, with a green skin and a pale green pulp that has a sharp, tangy flavor.

Buying & Storing

When choosing mangoes, select those that are shiny with unblemished skins. To test if they are ripe, gently squeeze them—they should give slightly to the touch. Avoid any fruit that looks mushy. Like many tropical fruits they will ripen in a warm room. If firm, they will keep for several weeks in a refrigerator or for about ten days at room temperature. The pureed pulp can be frozen.

Preparation & Cooking

To eat a fresh mango successfully you need to master the art of removing the pit. There are supposedly two methods of achieving this. The first is to cut round the center of the fruit, which in theory will enable you to twist the two halves apart in opposite directions and remove the pit easily. The mango has to be in a perfect condition for this procedure to be effective. What usually happens is that the juice spurts out from the fruit and splatters all over you!

The second method is to cut the mango along each side of the pit, leaving a rim of skin around the pit and providing two halves of pulp. Peel the skin off the pit and cut away or, better still, eat the pulp remaining on the pit. The two halves can either be eaten from the skin with a spoon or peeled, sliced, cubed, pureed or cut in hedgehogs.

To prepare mango hedgehogs, make crisscross cuts through the pulp without piercing the skin. Turn the skin inside out to form your hedgehogs.

Mangoes are perfect as a dessert fruit on their own and need no additions. They are, however, delicious in a fruit salad and make an appetizing starter, sliced with proscuitto. Added to palm hearts and avocado they make an unusual salad; mangoes are equally successful combined with shrimp.

Pureed mango can be made into ice creams, sorbets, fruit fools and tropical drinks—with or without alcohol. Diluted with a little lime juice, mango puree makes a stunning sauce with which to cover a dessert plate; arrange a pretty selection of thinly sliced tropical fruits on top. Mangoes can be cooked like apples in pudding and pies, and can also be candied and crystallized. In the West Indies they are often bottled with hot peppers in salted water and sold by the roadside as a spicy snack—pepper mangoes.

The unripe fruit is used a great deal in Indian and West Indian cooking to make pickles and chutneys; the raw pulp is sometimes dried and grated and used freely as a condiment in cooking (*Amchoor*).

Mangosteen

Mangosteen

Anyone who has ever eaten a mangosteen *(Garcinia mangostana)* is convinced that they have discovered the most exotic fruit in the world. This round dark purple-brown fruit looks rather like a smooth, small, oddly colored ball with sepals and a sturdy stalk on the top. It has a hard, almost leathery, thick skin, enclosing a waxy white pulp, which is divided in sections and shot with pale pink veins. Each section contains one or two seeds.

The juicy pulp of the mangosteen is similar to that of a lychee in texture, but the taste is quite different. It can best be described as delectable, sweet and fragrant. Some people compare its flavor to a cross between a grape and a peach, although even this description does not really do it justice.

Originally from Malaysia, this fruit is grown throughout Southeast Asia, the West Indies, Central America, Brazil and Florida. It is becoming increasingly available throughout the year.

Buying & Storing
Choose mangosteens that will yield slightly when pressed. Select the largest fruits available as they will contain the most pulp. Avoid any that look dry and feel very hard, as they will most likely have fermented inside. Mangosteens will store for up to two weeks in the refrigerator.

Preparation & Cooking
The skin is inedible—only the soft white pulp should be eaten. Mangosteens should be soft enough to be opened by hand, like a passion fruit. You can cut them open with a knife, but be careful not to cut too deep as there is a tannic juice in the skin which will affect the flavor of the pulp.

Treat mangosteens as a dessert fruit, eat raw by themselves, in fruit salads or with ice cream or whipped cream. In Indonesia, where they are plentiful, mangosteens are used in savory recipes for pickles and vinegars.

Avocado

Avocado slices make a perfect garnish

The pear-shaped avocado *(Persea americana)* is famed for its luscious pulp, with its creamy texture and subtle flavor. The avocado pulp is soft, oily and pale green. It is encased in a tough, dark-green to purple skin.

Originating in Mexico and South America, the first Europeans to see the avocado were the Spanish conquistadores when they invaded Mexico—the fruit had long been a staple of the Aztec diet. The name is in fact derived from the Aztec word *ahuacatl.* The avocado is a highly nutritious fruit, and has a much higher fat content that most other fruits, which only contain a trace of fat.

Today the avocado is grown all over the world in the tropics and subtropics. There are three basic categories of avocado—the Mexican, Guatemalan and West Indian. These three types have been crossed to produce over 500 varieties.

The most popular varieties are **Hass,** small with a wrinkly skin that turns brownish-purple as it ripens; **Fuerte,** large and elongated, with a smooth dark-green skin; **Nabal,** rounder-shaped with a smooth green skin turning reddish-brown when ripe and **Ettinger,** large, oblong-shaped with a shiny, thin, green skin. A relatively new development is the tiny cocktail avocado from Israel.

Buying & Storing

A ripe avocado will give slightly when pressed lightly at the top or bottom. Very bruised, soft fruits are usually over-ripe. It is best to buy firm fruit and allow to ripen at room temperature. Ripe fruit will keep in the refrigerator for up to four days.

Preparation & Cooking

The savory nature of the avocado makes it an ideal salad ingredient.

To prepare an avocado, cut in half lengthwise and gently pry out the pit. The pulp discolors very quickly, so brush cut surfaces with lemon juice to prevent them from browning. For avocado slices, peel back the skin, then slice.

The classic and probably best way to serve avocado is to fill the cavity with vinaigrette—the acidic contrast is delicious. Other good fillings include shellfish in mayonnaise; sour cream and chives; blue cheese dressing; or simply crushed garlic with lemon juice and black pepper.

Avocado pulp may be scooped out, chopped and mixed with poached fish in curried mayonnaise. The pulp blends very well with other ingredients to form dips—the most famous being *guacamole.* Avocado soup makes an unusual starter, while avocado ice cream and avocado filled with sweetened strawberries make different desserts.

Fuerte

Napal

Hass

Ettinger

Feijoa

The feijoa (*Feijoa sellowiana*) belongs to the *Myrtaceae* or myrtle family and is also known as Pineapple Guava. It is a round or oval fruit, about three inches long, with a thin waxy skin. It is similar in color and texture to the avocado.

The feijoa has a creamy-yellow colored grainy pulp with shiny black seeds. It is often mistaken for one of the guava family and, although it is a close relative, its tangy and aromatic flavor is closer to that of the passion fruit. It is rich in vitamin C.

Originally from South America, the feijoa was named after the botanist Don da silva Feijoa. The fruit was introduced into Europe in the 1890s and soon grew wild in the south of France. Today, the feijoa is cultivated in New Zealand (where it is very popular), Australia, Asia, Africa and the United States.

The fruit is harvested before it is ripe, kept to mature, and exported when it is at its best.

Buying & Storing

Select feijoa which yield slightly to the touch (like an avocado). When the pulp begins to soften, the fruit is ready. It will only store for a short period, so eat as soon as possible.

Preparation & Cooking

Feijoa should always be peeled. The fruit is perhaps best eaten raw on its own, but is also good in fruit salads, pureed and mixed with whipped cream, or made into a jam or jelly. Feijoa preserve is served with cold meats.

Guava

The guava (*Psidium guajava*) is a tropical fruit similar in appearance to a small quince. The fruits have a green or yellow skin which can be smooth or rough, depending on the species. Ideally guavas should not be picked until ripe. However, commercially grown guavas are picked when turning from green to yellow, so that they are ripe one day later. The pulp varies in color from white to yellow to pink, with an inner shell surrounding soft pulp which is full of small hard seeds.

Guavas have a strong characteristic aroma which can be overpowering. The flavor of this juicy fruit can best be described as sweet, acidic and exotic. The most common variety is the **Lemon Guava,** while the strawberry or **Purple Guava** (Psidium cattleianum), with its wine-colored skin and pulp, is perhaps regarded as the variety with the best flavor.

Originally from Mexico, Peru and Ecuador, the Spaniards and Portuguese brought guavas to the Philippines and coastal regions of India. From there they rapidly spread throughout the tropics and are now equally common in the subtropics, growing quite wild in some places. They are now grown in Australia, India, the West Indies, Africa, Hawaii and Brazil.

Guavas are one of the richest sources of vitamin C in fruit, containing up to ten times the amount found in citrus fruits.

Buying & Storing

Always choose guavas that are unblemished with a yellow skin, indicating that they are ripe. They should give slightly to the touch when gently pressed. Guavas have a very short shelf life, although they can be kept in cold storage for up to a week. Ideally they should be eaten as soon as they turn yellow. They should be stored away from other foods, and can be frozen.

Preparation & Cooking

It is always advisable to peel and seed guavas before eating or cooking them. They can be eaten raw by themselves or in a fruit salad. Guavas may also be cooked in a variety of ways: stewed in a compote; stuffed like apples; used in crisps; pureed and folded into whipped cream to make a light fruit fool; pickled to serve with meat. In South America and the West Indies guava cheese is a popular preserve. Guavas also make excellent jams and jellies.

Feijoa

Guava

Babaco

The babaco *(Carica pentagona)* looks similar to a large papaya and indeed is from the same family. It is becoming increasingly available. It ranges in color from green to bright-yellow, depending on ripeness, and weighs about two pounds. Its pulp is quite watery and crunchy, with a few soft seeds inside. The babaco has a unusual flavor—a mixture of lemon, banana and pineapple.

Until recently babaco was only found in Ecuador. Now it is cultivated in New Zealand and the Channel Islands. It is rich in vitamin C (two slices give your daily requirement).

Buying & Storing
Choose the fruit when it is turning bright-yellow—indicating that it is ripe. It should be uniformly soft. Babaco keep for up to a month in the refrigerator and several weeks in the open. If bad spots develop they can be cut out and will not spread.

Preparation & Cooking
All the fruit can be eaten; cut and use it as required. It should be consumed when yellow and fully ripened and makes a refreshing palate cleanser after a rich meal. When cut in slices, it has an attractive pentagonal shape. Treat in a similar way to the starfruit (carambola), sliced or cubed in fruit salad, stewed as a compote, made in preserves, or, as it is traditionally used in Equador, liquidized and made into a breakfast drink.

Papaya

The papaya or pawpaw *(Carica papaya)* is one of the fastest growing tropical fruits. Papayas vary a great deal in size and shape. They can be as small as a large pear or as large as an elongated melon. The skin ranges from green when unripe, through to yellow and orange.

When cut open the papaya resembles a melon in that it has soft juicy pulp surrounding a star-shaped cavity. This is full of gelatinous black seeds, which are generally discarded but can be eaten in small amounts, as they have a hot flavor—similar to mustard and cress. The pulp is orange or pink, softer than a melon but with a similar texture, and is very sweet with a slightly perfumed flavor.

Papayas were originally grown in the Caribbean islands—the name papaya comes from the Carib word *ababai*. Today they grow prodigiously throughout the tropics and subtropics; they are even cultivated in the Channel Islands.

The papaya tree grows up to 25 feet high and the fruit resembles gigantic Brussel sprouts, clustered around the stalk of the plant under the leaves. The fruit contains an enzyme—papain—which has the ability to break down protein, and is widely used as a meat tenderizer. Pectin is found in unripe papaya. The raw fruit is renowned for its digestive properties, and it is a good source of vitamin C—containing more than oranges.

Buying & Storing
When choosing papayas select those that are firm and unblemished. The color may vary from green to yellow to orange with a few freckles, but avoid any with soft patches. Ripe papayas will give slightly. To speed up ripening, put in a paper bag with a banana in a dark place. Papaya is not suitable for freezing.

Preparation & Cooking
To prepare the ripe fruit, cut in half lengthwise and scoop out the seeds. Cut away the thin skin, then cut in slices or cubes, or puree.

The best way to serve papayas is on their own, with perhaps a squeeze of lime juice, or with proscuitto. They also make delicious additions to fruit salads, savory salads, sorbets or fruit fools. They can be liquidized and made into unusual salad dressings and drinks.

The unripe fruit may be cooked in the same way as summer squash, stuffed with spiced meat and baked. It can be added to soups and stews or made into pickles and chutneys.

Babaco

Papaya

Starfruit (Carambola)

The starfruit or carambola (*Averrhoa carambola*), also known as the star apple, has recently found its way into our large supermarkets and specialist green grocers. It resembles a small pointed lantern about three to five inches long with a green or yellow, thin, waxy skin. When cut in slices crosswise, it looks like a five-sided star—hence its popular name. The translucent juicy pulp is yellow or orange with a crunchy texture and a sharp aromatic flavor. It can best be described as juicy, refreshing and slightly acidic. The pulp contains small oval seeds which should be removed once the fruit is sliced.

Originally from Malaysia and Indonesia this popular fruit is now found throughout the tropics. It is also being cultivated in the United States and Brazil. There is a smaller relative called the **Bilimbi** or cucumber tree fruit (*Averrhoa bilimbi*), which looks similar having the same shape and color, but is slightly smaller and greener. The bilimbi is too sour to be eaten raw. They both belong to the wood sorrel family, and are rich in vitamin C.

Buying & Storing
Buy firm unblemished fruit that is ripe. In the case of the starfruit, this may vary in color from greenish-yellow to bright-yellow to almost orange. The bilimbi remains greenish-yellow. Both keep up to a week in the refrigerator or several days at room temperature. They will ripen at room temperature. Both fruits are very fragile so handle them carefully. The larger fruits tend to be sweeter than the smaller ones.

Preparation & Cooking
The whole starfruit is edible. Sometimes the ridges along the sides may be a little tough; if so, cut them off, then slice the fruit horizontally and remove the seeds. When ripe, sliced starfruit is an attractive addition to a fruit or savory salad. It can be eaten on its own as a refreshing dessert fruit, liquidized and made into a thirst-quenching drink, sauce or jam. The starfruit can also be stewed, preserved or pickled.

The less sweet bilimbi is generally cooked with sugar and made in a compote, or preserved in salt, vinegar or sugar syrup, or added to chutney.

Sapote (Sapodilla)

The sapote or sapodilla (*Achras sapota*), also known as the naseberry, chicku and tree potato, is one of the increasing number of tropical fruits that are now available. Sapodillas are small, round or oval brown fruits, about the size of a kiwifruit. In appearance they look a cross between a kiwi and a small potato with a roughish skin which smooths out as the fruit ripens. The pulp is brown and granular, like a pear, with several large black hooked seeds in the center which are easily removed. When ripe they taste like toffee or brown sugar—very sweet.

Sapotes grow wild in the forests of southern Mexico and can be traced back to the time of the Aztecs and Mayans through their carvings on sapote wood. Today they are cultivated all over the tropics—in India, Southeast Asia, the West Indies, Israel and tropical areas of America.

Buying & Storing
When choosing sapotes you can tell if they are ripe if they are soft to the touch and if the skin shows yellow when scratched; if unripe the scratch will be green. Sapotes will however ripen in a warm room. Always ensure the fruit is ripe as an immature fruit is virtually inedible. Unripe fruit will keep for at least six weeks in a refrigerator, and ripe fruit also keeps well if refrigerated.

Preparation & Cooking
Either cut the sapote in half and scoop out the pulp with a spoon, using the skins—which are not eaten—as shells, or peel and cut in slices. Discard the seeds.

Sapotes are generally eaten as a dessert fruit with a squeeze of lime juice. They can also be added sliced to a fruit salad, or pureed and made into a fruit fool, ice cream or sorbet.

Durian

*Starfruit
(Carambola)*

*Sapote
(Sapodilla)*

Durian

The durian *(Durio zibethinus)* is worth mentioning even though it is unlikely you may have the opportunity to taste it, for it is a curious fruit. It looks a little like a jack fruit and can weigh from 4-1/2 pounds to 10 pounds. It is oval in shape, and covered with sharp spikes which are either green or yellow. Once cut open it reveals a thick rind, enclosing creamy colored soft pulp which is divided in three to five sections, each containing large brown seeds.

The most remarkable characteristic of this fruit is its smell. It is foul and has often been compared to rotten eggs and worse. Apparently the taste does not reflect its aroma but resembles a sweet, rich, aromatic custard. It is native to Malaysia and Indonesia and is also cultivated in Thailand. It is rarely found outside these countries as the smell prevents it being exported successfully.

Buying & Storing
Do not choose any fruit that has split open as this indicates that it is overripe. Keep away from other food.

Preparation & Cooking
Cut in half with a serrated knife and scoop out the pulp with a spoon. The seeds can also be eaten if roasted or boiled. In its native country it is eaten fresh as a dessert fruit. It is also used in cakes, ice creams and preserves. Before it is ripe it is cooked as a vegetable.

Custard Apples

The *Annona* trees produce a variety of delicious fruits which are generally known as custard apples. All the fruits in this family are multiple fruits, made up of sections that grow together. The pulp is soft, suggesting the consistency of custard, and it is full of shiny, black seeds.

Most of the *annona* fruits originated in the American tropics, but nowadays they are cultivated in places like Asia, Australia, Spain and, in particular, Israel. The cherimoya began its history in Peru, where it is regarded as one of the finest fruits in the world.

Cherimoya: The most commonly known, and arguably best, species. The skin of the cherimoya *(Annona cherimolia)* is greenish-grey with a scaled pattern. The white pulp is sweet and perfumed, forming a natural custard in its own right.

Sugar Apple: Often regarded as the true custard apple, this fruit *(Annona squamosa),* is sweeter than the cherimoya. It has a yellowish-green skin, which is made up of strange fleshy scales. When fully ripe, the scales burst open to reveal a creamy pulp, which is extremely sweet and slightly grainy.

Soursop: Larger than the other types, the soursop *(Annona muricata)* can weigh up to eight ounces. The thin skin has rows of dark-green, curved spines and the white pulp has a refreshing, sour-sweet flavor, more acidic than the other *annona* fruits.

Bullock's Heart: Not as good in flavor as the others. The appearance of bullock's heart *(Annona reticulata)* is suggested by its name. It has a brownish-red skin with a scaly surface and the pulp is sweet and granular.

Atemoya: A fruit with great potential, the atemoya *(Annona atemoya)* is a cross between the cherimoya and the sugar apple. It was developed in Florida. The pulp is sweet-tasting and the skin is light-green and bumpy. This fruit travels well.

Buying & Storing:
When buying *annona* fruit, be careful not to pierce the surprisingly delicate skin. Choose slightly soft fruit—the fruit can be ripened in a dark room for a few days and may be refrigerated for a short time.

Preparation & Cooking:
The delicious pulp of *annona* fruit is best eaten raw and slightly chilled. Simply halve or quarter the fruit and scoop out the pulp with a spoon. The seeds are not eaten, so the pulp is quite often sieved to remove them. This produces a sweet puree which can be served as an aromatic custard.

Combined with a little whipped cream, the puree makes a delicious fruit fool. It also makes a tasty ice cream and sorbet, and is an excellent addition to trifles, soufflés and mousses.

Watered down and pepped up with a little lemon or lime juice, and sugar, the puree forms an exotic milk shake.

Jack Fruit

The jack fruit *(Artocarpus heterophyllus)* is one of the world's largest cultivated fruits, weighting up to 90 pounds. As the fruit ripens, the skin turns from green to brown and is covered with blunt spines. The pockets of pulp hold a number of large white seeds; the pulp itself is succulent and has a distinctive aroma which is extremely strong when the fruit is ripe.

Native to India, the jack fruit is now grown in most tropical areas, but it is especially popular in Southeast Asia. The tender fruit is either eaten raw or cooked in various sweet and savory dishes. In Asia, sliced jack fruit is sometimes used in curries or turned into confections and condiments.

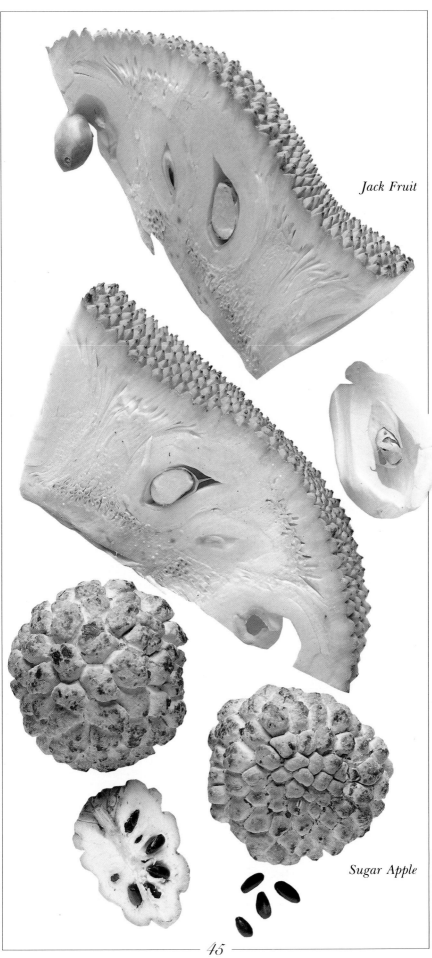

Jack Fruit

Sugar Apple

Lychee

Lychee

An aromatic oriental fruit, the lychee *(Litchi chinensis)* has a most unusual skin. When ripe, the fruit is about the size of a small plum and has a red, rough-textured, leathery skin. After a few days, this skin becomes brittle and turns reddish-brown.

The skin is easily removed, to reveal a pearly-white pulp, surrounding a brown, shiny pit. At first bite, the pulp appears to be slightly dry, but on eating, it melts in a fragrant juiciness.

The lychee originated in China and has been cultivated there for at least 2,000 years: it has always been prized by the Chinese. Thailand and the Philippines have also cultivated lychees for centuries. But today the fruit also grows in India, South Africa, the United States, New Zealand, Japan and Australia. The fruit is a good source of vitamin C.

Buying & Storing

Look for firm fruit with a definite pink tinge, and make sure that the skins are not broken. Lychees will keep refrigerated for about two weeks; they also freeze well—put the unshelled fruit in a freezer bag and freeze for up to three months.

Preparation & Cooking

To prepare lychees, simply break open the brittle skin, press gently and pop out the white fruit. To fully appreciate the delicate, perfumed flavor of the lychee, it is best to serve the fruit whole and slightly chilled. As a rather splendid dessert, serve a pile of peeled lychees on a bed of ice.

The fruit also adds an exotic touch to fruit salads and is lovely served with ginger-flavored ice cream or brandy-flavored whipped cream.

The scented flavor of lychees makes them an excellent ingredient for Chinese sweet and sour or stir-fried dishes, while a Chinese-style salad of lychees and cold chicken is quite delicious. The fruit also makes an interesting water-ice. Dried lychees are known as Chinese nuts.

Longan

An oriental fruit, related to the lychee, the longan *(Nephelium longana)* is a round fruit, about one inch in diameter. The thin, brittle skin ranges in color from brown to yellowish-red and is often covered in tiny bumps. The semitranslucent pulp within is similar in texture to the lychee, and once bitten into is juicy and sweet. Flavor-wise it is somewhat similar to a grape, but much more aromatic. The pulp encloses a shiny brown pit.

Originating in India, the longan is now commonly grown alongside the lychee in China. It has the benefit of ripening when the lychee season is over.

When buying longans, look for firm, unsplit skins. Prepare and use in the same way as lychees.

Pulasan

The pulasan *(Nephelium mutabile)* is related to the lychee, but has a skin covered in short red or yellow projections. Like the lychee, the skin comes away from the fruit very easily, but the pulp is firmly attached to the pit. The pulp is sweet, juicy and strongly scented. Producer countries are predominantly the Philippines and Indonesia.

Prepare and use pulasan in the same way as the lychee.

Rambutan

The rambutan *(Nephelium lappaceum)* is also related to the lychee. The striking feature of this fruit is its skin, which is covered with red or yellow soft spines. This unusual skin is broken open to reveal a white, juicy fruit which has the same texture as the lychee but is slightly less aromatic. The pulp is firmly attached to a long seed.

Native to Malaysia, the name is derived from the Malay word *rambut*, meaning hair. Very much a tropical fruit, the rambutan is very popular in Southeast Asia, where it is often grown in gardens or small orchards. It is now beginning to be produced commercially for Western countries.

The fruit does not contain as much vitamin C as the lychee.

Buying & Storing
When buying rambutans, look for firm fruit. The ripe fruit will not keep for long.

Preparation & Cooking
To prepare, hold the fruit over a bowl, cut open the skin with a knife, then peel. A small quantity of sweet juice will be released when the fruit is first cut.

The refreshing pulp is best served raw in the same way as the lychee. A striking way to serve rambutans is to cut away only half of the skin so that the fruit looks as it is nestling in strange, spiky containers. The scented pulp is a natural addition to tropical fruit salads, especially when flavored with liqueur or brandy.

Rambutan

Orange

Shamouti

The orange, with its juicy pulp, vivid color and flavor-filled skin, is one of the world's most versatile fruits. All oranges originally came from China, but their history is somewhat hazy. It is likely that they were first brought to Italy from Asia by Arab traders, towards the end of the Roman Empire. These early oranges were bitter-tasting.

The sweet eating oranges were first brought to Europe by the Portuguese explorers.

The smaller loose-skinned oranges, which are generally grouped as mandarins or tangerines, were introduced to Europe during the early 19th century; they evolved from the sweet-tasting oranges.

SWEET ORANGE

The sweet orange *(Citrus sinensis)*, with its brightly-colored thick skin and soft juicy pulp, is delicious.

Today sweet oranges are grown in almost every country with a warm climate, but the most prolific crops come from Spain, Israel, South Africa and southern United States.

Navel: So called because it has a characteristic circular mark at one end, this is a fine, almost seedless orange. It is easy to peel and segment, and is very juicy.

Valencia: Another favorite, which is a late variety with a long season. A small juicy orange with a fairly smooth skin, the Valencia is excellent for eating fresh and for making juice.

Shamouti: This is the original Jaffa orange, and has a good flavor.

Blood Orange: This has a skin flecked with red, and a reddish pulp that is sweet and full of flavor.

BITTER ORANGE

Bitter oranges *(Citrus aurantium)* have a rough dark-orange skin which is aromatic. The seed-filled pulp is too sour to be eaten raw.

The first bitter oranges imported into Britain came from Spain and were called Seville after the town that grew and exported them round Europe. They are still cultivated for marmalade, although nowadays Sicily exports many Seville-style bitter oranges.

The oil extracted from bitter oranges is used as the basic flavoring for liqueurs such as Curaçao, Grand Marnier and Cointreau. Bitter orange trees are also grown in the Mediterranean for their flowers, which are used for orange flower water, as well as perfume.

Blood Orange

Navel

Valencia

Seville

Celmentine

Ortanique

Topaz

Satsuma

Mandarins & Tangerines

Mandarins and tangerines (*Citrus reticulata*) are traditionally served at Christmas time, when it is their peak harvesting season. They have characteristic loose skins which are easy to remove. The pulp is usually sweet and juicy, making them ideal dessert fruit. There are many varieties and the species is frequently crossed with other fruit to produce unusual hybrids. The terms mandarin and tangerine are interchangeable.

Satsuma: One of the best known varieties, originating in Japan. It has sweet pulp which is almost always seedless, and is a popular early season variety.

Clementine: This has an outstandingly good flavor. It was originated in North Africa and is a cross between the mandarin and bitter Seville orange. Again seedless, the fruits are known as oh-my-darlings in the fruit trade.

Dancy: An American cross between the mandarin and sweet orange, this is another good fruit, with an aromatic flavor.

Minneola: A bell-shaped fruit with a slightly bitter-sweet flavor, this was produced by crossing a mandarin with a grapefruit.

Wilkins: A fruit grown in the Mediterranean, which—like the minneola—is being introduced to extend the mandarin season.

Temple and **Topaz:** Two other hybrids which are now commonly seen.

Ortanique: A popular West Indian fruit, this is probably a cross between a tangerine and a sweet orange. It is more the size of an orange, but slightly flattened in shape and very juicy and sweet.

Buying & Storing
Choose fruit which is bright, glossy and unblemished. Skins should be loose, but not squashy. Store oranges in a cool place; mandarins and tangerines do not keep as well as tight-skinned oranges.

Preparation & Cooking

Orange segments and slices, juice and peel are used extensively in cooking. The juice is easily extracted with a squeezer.

To remove the outer layer (peel), thinly pare with a potato peeler in a downwards motion. For julienne strips, cut the pared peel in thin strips with a sharp knife and blanch for use as a garnish. Alternatively, use a zester to make much finer strips which do not need blanching.

Finely grate the peel to use for flavoring, or rub the skin with a sugar lump to extract the oil.

To peel an orange right down to the pulp, slice off the ends and, using a sawing motion, cut off the peel in a spiral, removing as much pith as possible. The orange is now ready for slicing or sectioning.

To make perfect sections, freeze the peeled orange 10 minutes, then, using a sharp knife, cut down between the membranes and remove the skinless sections.

Classic orange desserts include the Italian caramelized oranges, orange and chocolate mousse, and Crêpes Suzette. Orange sections soaked in syrup flavored with orange peel and liqueur are delicious. Oranges combine well with strawberries and rhubarb, and they are a natural choice for ice creams, sorbets and jellies.

Whole mandarins—clementines in particular—are delicious canned in liqueur-flavored syrup.

Orange juice and grated peel are used for flavoring cakes, cookies and icings, while the strips of peel are used for infusing syrups. Dried mandarin peel is a popular flavoring in Chinese cooking. Candied orange peel is delicious dipped in chocolate or used for decoration.

Orange segments are included in winter salads—such as endive and orange salad. Soups marrying orange with carrots or tomatoes are most refreshing, and butter flavored with orange peel and juice complements grilled meat. Liver is enhanced with an orange sauce.

Bitter oranges are generally better for cooked savory dishes. They are used to make Bigarade sauce, the traditional accompaniment for duck, and they are a good foil for rich lamb or beef. In the Mediterranean, dried strips of orange peel are used in bouquet garni. But, of course, the main use for Seville oranges is marmalade.

Julienne strips, twists of peel and orange sections for decoration

Grapefruit

Loved by slimmers, but somewhat maligned by cooks, the grapefruit (*Citrus paradisi*) has a deliciously bitter-sweet pulp. It is one of the largest of the citrus fruits. The grapefruit has a skin ranging in color from greenish-yellow to blushing-pink. The pulp is usually pale-yellow, apart from the pink-skinned grapefruit which has reddish pulp to match the skin. The pink varieties are sweeter than the yellow ones. The fruit grows in clusters, rather like an outsize bunch of grapes, hence the name grapefruit.

Thought to be an offshoot of the pomelo, the grapefruit first appeared in the West Indies during the 18th century. From there it traveled to Florida, where it was first produced on a commercial basis. The United States is still the main producer. Grapefruit is also grown in South America and in Mediterranean countries, Israel and Cyprus in particular.

Buying & Storing

Select fruit which has a shiny lustre—a sign of freshness—and no soft spots. It should feel heavy for its size—a good indication of juiciness. Grapefruit will store for up to two weeks in the refrigerator.

Preparation and Cooking

To prepare grapefruit, halve crosswise and use a grapefruit knife to separate the pulp from the skin, then slice between the sections and their membranes, to loosen. The pulp can then be scooped out easily with a spoon.

To peel a grapefruit, cut a slice from the stem end, then cut downwards to remove the peel in strips. Scrape off any remaining pith, which is very bitter. Cut between the membranes to remove perfect segments.

The halved fruit makes a classic starter, sprinkled with sugar or ground ginger. It is also delicious sprinkled with dry sherry or vermouth and grilled until bubbling. As a refreshing snack, mix grapefruit sections with cottage cheese and roasted almonds. Candied grapefruit peel is particularly good.

Serve grapefruit sorbet or water ice in the scooped-out shells, and use the fruit with other citrus fruit to make excellent marmalade.

Pomelo

The largest of all citrus fruits, the pomelo (*Citrus grandis*) has a thick, yellowish-green skin and a rather dry, bitter-sweet pulp.

The fruit is native to Malaysia and is probably an ancestor of the grapefruit. Rather confusingly, it is also known as Shaddock, after the East India captain who left seeds in Barbados on his way back to England. It is grown for local consumption in Southeast Asia and is now exported from Israel.

Pomelos will store in a cool place for a couple of weeks. Serve peeled and segmented as a change from grapefruit. The peel is ideal for candying.

Ugli

A cross between a grapefruit and a tangerine, the ugli (*Citrus reticulata X C. paradisi*) is about the same size as the grapefruit, but has an uneven, greenish-orange skin. In looks, it lives up to its name, yet the pulp is juicy and pleasant, with a taste that is halfway between a tangerine and a grapefruit. The skin is quite loose, making the fruit easy to peel.

As with grapefruit, uglis should feel heavy for their size as an indication of juiciness, and kept in a cool place. Uglis are delicious served simply peeled and sectioned; as for grapefruit, remove all membranes. The flavor of ugli blends well in fruit salads.

Grapefruit

Pink
Grapefruit

Pomelo

Ugli

Lemon

The versatile lemon *(Citrus limon)* has a multitude of culinary uses. The familiar bright-yellow fruit, with its sharp-tasting juice, is thought to have originated in India but its history is rather vague. Brought to Europe by the Arabs, the lemon probably became popular during the 12th century. Today the lemon is widely grown in frost-free Mediterranean countries, such as Italy, Spain, Cyprus and Israel. California is also a prolific grower of lemons.

Although there are many varieties of lemon, they are rarely sold under their varietal names. The smaller, smooth-skinned varieties tend to be juicier than the larger, coarse-skinned type. They are all extremely rich in vitamin C.

Buying & Storing
Select glossy, firm fruit. Whole lemons will keep refrigerated for about two weeks; cut lemons should be wrapped in plastic wrap and used as quickly as possible. They are available year around, so there seems little point in freezing them. However, lemon slices frozen in ice cubes may come in handy for flavoring drinks.

Preparation & Cooking
Lemon pulp is far too sour to be eaten by itself, but the freshly squeezed juice and the tangy peel play vital culinary roles.

To extract the maximum amount of juice from a lemon, bring it to room temperature, then roll on the work surface for a few minutes, before squeezing.

To remove strips of peel, pare thinly with a potato peeler in a downwards motion; cut in thin strips to make julienne strips. Alternatively, use a zester to make ultra-thin shreds. Boil lemon strips in water until softened before using. Finely grate the peel to use as a flavoring.

To prepare perfect lemon slices for garnishing, first chill the fruit then, using a very sharp knife, cut in slices or wedges. For decorative slices, groove the lemon lengthwise with a canelle knife before slicing.

To make a lemon twist, cut a lemon slice from the center to the edge, then open, twisting the points in opposite directions.

To make a butterfly garnish, arrange two quarter slices with a parsley sprig in the middle.

Lemon juice is rich in citric acid and is often used as a souring agent in western cooking. It is also brushed on cut fruit—like avocados, apples and bananas—to prevent discoloration. Lemon juice can also be added to the water when boiling root vegetables to preserve their color.

Lemon juice is used in salad dressings and emulsion sauces, such as hollandaise. The tangy peel gives a lift to stuffings, cakes and syrups. Lemon has a special affinity with fish. In Greece, lemon juice is mixed with egg yolk to make the classic *avgolemono.*

Lemon meringue pie, lemon soufflé and syllabub are classic desserts. Lemon curd is a traditional English preserve, while spicy pickled lemons from the East are delicious served with cold meat.

Fresh lemonade and the French *citron pressé*—lemon juice, a little sugar and water—are deliciously refreshing drinks.

Citron

In appearance, the citron *(Citrus medica)* resembles a large bumpy lemon. The first citrus fruit to reach Europe from the Far East, citrons are cultivated for their thick aromatic skin which is usually candied. Most citrons come from the Mediterranean.

Lemons & garnishes

Kumquat

A tiny fruit, the kumquat has a thin, sweet-tasting skin and bittersweet pulp, which usually contains many small seeds. Although not strictly a citrus fruit, the kumquat closely resembles a small orange in appearance and taste.

Originating in China, the name is derived from the Chinese *kam kwat*, meaning gold-orange. There are two major varieties: the oval kumquat (*Fortunella margarita*) and the round kumquat (*Fortunella japonica*). The fruit is cultivated in several countries, including Japan, Israel, Spain and Malaysia.

Recently the fruit has been crossed with citrus fruits to create limequat, citrangequat and orangequat. The calamondin is another small orange-like fruit, used in Philippine cooking which may well be a cross between the kumquat and the mandarin.

Buying & Storing
Buy firm, shiny fruit—avoid blemished specimens. Fruit with green tinges will ripen at home. Store ripe kumquats at room temperature for up to four days or refrigerate for a week.

Preparation & Cooking
The delight of the kumquat is that it can be eaten whole. Simply remove the stem and slice in half lengthwise if desired.

Kumquats are wonderful preserved in a syrup or brandy. They also make tangy pickles or relishes, and piquant sauces for meat and poultry.

Whole fruit can be transformed instantly into delectable confections by simply coating in fondant, caramel or chocolate. Sliced kumquats make an attractive decoration for desserts and cakes.

Lime

The small round lime (*Citrus aurantifolia*) is similar to the lemon, but has a thinner skin and is bright-green in color. The pale-green pulp produces a sharp juice which contains about one-third more citric acid than a large lemon; the juice has a much spicier fragrance than that of the lemon.

Native to Southeast Asia, limes prefer a hotter, damper climate than lemons and they flourish in the tropics, where they replace lemons. The Arabs brought the lime westwards—in fact, the name lime comes from the Arabic word *limah* (as does lemon). Lime juice was also given to sailors to prevent scurvy, hence the sailors nickname limeys.

There are two main types of lime generally available—the Caribbean type is large and very green, while the Indian is smaller, more yellowish-green in color and very sour in taste. Major producers include the United States, Brazil, Mexico, Israel, Egypt and the West Indies.

Buying & Storing
Choose firm, smooth-skinned limes, avoiding any shriveled or wrinkled fruit. Store in the refrigerator for up to three weeks. Whole limes will keep in the freezer for up to eight months.

Preparation & Cooking
Limes are prepared and used for cooking in the same way as lemons, although limes have rather more fragrance. If substituting lime juice for lemon juice in a recipe, reduce the amount by about one-third.

Lime garnishes are just as stunning as lemon ones. The juice is used a great deal in cocktails and lime slices and twists of lime peel are often added to drinks.

Lime marinades for fish are most effective. The preserving powers of lime juice are well illustrated in the Mexican pickled fish dish *seviche*. Key lime pies are a Florida specialty and lime sorbet and mousse are deliciously refreshing.

Kumquat

Lime

Orangequat

Grape

Seedless varieties

One of the oldest cultivated fruits, grapes *(Vitis vinifera)* have been grown for literally thousands of years, mainly to produce wine. The clusters of small fruit have an aura of luxury.

Grapes probably originated in western Asia and were first introduced to Italy and France by the early Greeks. The Romans developed viticulture to a high standard and vineyards flourished throughout Roman-dominated Europe.

During the 1870s, the pest known as *phylloxera,* almost completely wiped out European grapes until it was discovered that the native American vine was immune to the pest. Virtually all the European vines had to be grafted onto American rootstocks in order to make them resistant to the bug.

Although still grown predominantly for wine, the grape is also a very popular dessert fruit. The varieties classified as dessert grapes tend to be larger and sweeter than wine grapes, but some varieties are used for both purposes. Certain types of grapes are also dried to produce raisins, while others are processed into nonalcoholic juice.

Today grapes are grown in all countries with a warm, sunny climate. Main producers of dessert grapes include California, Australia, South Africa, Chile, Israel, Italy and Spain. Nowadays some of the more succulent grapes are grown in greenhouses, particularly in Belgium.

Generally, all grapes are distinguished by color: either black or white. It is purely the skin that gives the grape its color. Beneath the skin of both types the pulp is white, although black-skinned grapes may have a pinkish flush—this turns white on cooking. The flavor depends to a great extent on the skins too; the tannin content will determine how astringent the skin will taste.

Flavor varies according to where the grapes are grown, since they are very sensitive to soil and climate. The best grapes will be delicately scented and tender. Most varieties have seeds, although seedless varieties are quite popular.

WHITE GRAPES

In reality white grapes vary in color from pale-green to amber-yellow. Among the dessert grapes available, the amber-green **Muscat** is renowned for its sweet flavor and musky aroma. The musky-scented **Italia** is a delicious large grape. The **Almeria,** also known as Ohanes, is another popular variety; it is large and has firm pulp.

Seedless white grapes, such as **Californian Seedless,** are now very popular; **Sultanas** are a classic variety, while the related **Thompson Seedless** are an important American variety. They are small, pale-green grapes with a sweet, yet refreshing taste.

BLACK GRAPES

Black grapes vary in color from deep rose-pink to purple and black.

Muscat

Italia

Almeria

California Seedless

Thompson Seedless

Frosted grapes

Alphonse Lavallée is a large blue-black grape with juicy pulp and a tender skin. Another juicy blue-black variety is **Royal,** while **Cardinal** is a redder color and has a sweet, musky flavor.

Black Hamburg is a well known type of grape grown in hot-houses—the grapes are fat, juicy and extremely fragrant. **Black Beauty** is a juicy, seedless grape from the United States. **Flame** is a delicious new seedless variety.

Buying & Storing

The grapes that are widely available in the shops have been cultivated for eating. They are very delicate and should be handled with care—try to avoid damaging the bloom or translucent film that surrounds each grape. The best grapes will be sold protected by tissue paper.

Avoid grapes with the slightest trace of browning around the stalk. Highly perishable, grapes will only stay at their peak for up to 48 hours. If they are not to be eaten immediately, store loosely wrapped in a cool place.

Preparation & Cooking

The perfect accompaniment to cheese, dessert grapes are a pure pleasure to eat. Just before serving, gently wash in cold water and let dry on paper towels.

The sweet flavor and attractive shape make grapes a popular ingredient in cooking, and for decoration. They usually need to be peeled and seeded.

To peel grapes, dip them in boiling water, then peel back the skin with your fingers. To seed grapes, hook out the seeds with a hairpin or make a slit in one side and flick out the seeds.

Frosted grapes make lovely decorations: cut the grapes in small bunches, then dip into lightly beaten egg white. Shake off the excess and dip into superfine sugar to coat. Dry on waxed paper for two to three hours.

Fresh grapes lend themselves to all sorts of sweet and savory fruit salads, while unpeeled and halved they make an attractive topping for tarts or cheesecakes. A classic French tart features black and white grapes, arranged alternately in concentric circles, on top of crème pâtissière. Grapes set in a molded jelly in another effective and ancient culinary delight. Grapes also make a delicious brûlée.

The delicate flavor of grapes combines well with white meat or fish—a white wine sauce, flavored with grapes is the basis for the classic Sole Véronique.

Peeled grapes also combine well with chicken in a salad, or try them with cucumber and scallops—dressed with a mint-flavored vinaigrette—as an original starter. Surprisingly, grapes also go well with game, such as pheasant.

Large white grapes can be halved and sandwiched back together with creamed blue cheese flavored with port—to make interesting cocktail nibbles.

Vine leaves are of course also used for cooking; stuffed with rice, meat and pine nuts, they are transformed into Greek *dolmades.*

Cardinal

Flame

Royal

Melon

*Attractive orange-pulp melons are
ideal for scooping in balls*

The sweet melon (*Cucumis melo*) is a popular fruit; its name is derived from Greek and means big apple. It is a member of the cucumber squash family; the watermelon belongs to a different family.

Melons were first cultivated in ancient Egypt, only reaching Europe during the Renaissance. Today the melon is cultivated all over the world—Israel, Spain, Portugal, all the Mediterranean countries, South America, South Africa, Mexico, Chile, southern United States, southeast Europe and Holland, and the Middle-East—all producing excellent quality fruit.

There are many different kinds of melon to choose from. They vary in size and shape, color and taste, but all melons have a soft, sweet, juicy pulp. The most widely available varieties are as follows:

Winter Melons: These include the **Honeydew** and the **Lavan** or Honeyball. Honeydew melons are generally oval-shaped with a hard green, white or yellow skin, often ribbed, depending on the variety. The pulp is pale, green to pink. It has an unremarkable flavor; its main virtue is that it is sweet, quite inexpensive and available throughout the winter.

The lavan melon is similar to the

honeydew, but rounder in shape and with a more pronounced flavor.

Musk, Netted or **Nutmeg Melons:** This type of melon is distinguished by a creamy-colored raised netting that covers the skin, which may also be segmented. It can be round or oval with an aromatic pink, orange or green pulp. The most popular example of this variety is the small round **Galia** melon from Israel, which has a green skin that turns to brownish-yellow when ripe.

Ogen Melon: A small round melon which originated in Israel and is now cultivated throughout the world. It has a bright-yellow, thinnish skin with distinctive green stripes and aromatic, succulent, green pulp.

Charentais Melon: One of the best varieties available in Europe, grown mainly in France. It has a green skin with a sweet orange pulp and a distinctive perfumed flavor.

Cantaloupe Melon: This has a scaly bumpy skin, which is sometimes grooved. Cantaloupe pulp can be green but is more often orange, with a strong sweet fragrant taste when ripe. These melons are widely grown in Europe and the United States.

Lavan

Honeydew

Charentais

Galia

Ogen

Cantaloupe

Tiger Melon: A relatively new variety from Turkey. It has orange, yellow and black stripes—hence the name—and soft, almost apple-flavored pulp.

Buying & Storing

Whatever the variety, melons must be eaten when they are perfectly ripe for optimum flavor. This is not always easy to assess when buying melons, especially if the particular variety has a thick hard skin, such as some honeydews.

The small varieties—ogen, cantaloupe and charentais—should smell of their own perfume and yield slightly when gently pressed at the stem end. In general, melons should feel heavy for their size.

Most melons store well and can be kept for a few days at room temperature until they are ripe and then in the refrigerator (wrap in plastic wrap as the smell tends to permeate other foods). The large honeydew melons can keep for a few weeks; the smaller varieties should be eaten as soon as they are ripe. Melon is not suitable for freezing.

Preparation & Cooking

When perfectly ripe, sweet melons are best served chilled, just as they are. The more perfumed varieties can be served with a squeeze of lemon or lime juice, sherry or port. They can also be flavored with ginger. The melon pulp can be sliced, diced, or made in balls, then served in scooped-out melon skins. The hollowed-out skins also make useful containers for fruit salads, ice creams and sorbets.

Melon with proscuitto is a classic starter. The fruit is also delicious in fruit and savory salads. Melons make excellent sorbets and are sometimes served as a cold soup. Pureed melon can be made in a thick sweet drink—good for daiquiris and fruit punches.

Watermelon

The watermelon *(Citrullus vulgaris)* is a large fruit, weighing up to 20 pounds, although smaller varieties, such as **Sweet Baby,** are being cultivated commercially. Watermelons are either round or oval-shaped with a smooth, shiny skin, which may be plain dark-green, light-green or yellow, mottled or striped. The crisp juicy pulp is usually red though there is a creamy-pulp variety **(Yellow Baby).** The pulp is surrounded by a white inner rind which may be up to two inches thick.

Originally from Africa, the watermelon has been cultivated for over 4,000 years and is now grown in tropical and subtropical regions all over the world.

Buying & Storing

When choosing a watermelon, the best way to tell if it is ripe is to cut out a little triangle and taste it—this is common practice in many of the countries in which it is grown. As this method is unlikely to be popular in supermarkets, a general guide is to choose those that are firm and evenly colored, apart from a lighter strip where they may have been lying on the ground. The rind should look soft and waxy. It is easier to select when the fruit is already cut. The pulp should be firm, crisp and bright-colored, not dry. Watermelons can be stored in the refrigerator wrapped in plastic wrap for up to a week.

Preparation & Cooking

The best way to serve watermelon is ice cold straight from the refrigerator. It is the most thirst-quenching of all fruits and is usually served simply cut in wedges. Alternatively, it can be cut from the rind, seeded and cubed, or shaped in balls with a melon baller, and served in the hollowed-out shell.

Watermelon is delicious mixed with shrimp and a spicy cocktail sauce, or combined with other fruit and vegetables in sweet and savory salads. It can be liquidized and made in exotic drinks and refreshing sorbets and ice creams. Frozen cubes of watermelon make excellent substitutes for frozen pops. The fruit can be hollowed out and the shell carved, wrapped in plastic wrap and frozen for later use as a natural container for fruit desserts.

Sweet Baby

Watermelon

Kiwifruit

Celebrated for its attractive pulp, the kiwifruit *(Actinidia chinensis)* is now a familiar fruit. Its fuzzy, brownish, thin skin hides a juicy, brilliant-green pulp which has an elongated cream-colored core, surrounded by tiny black seeds. When sliced across, this arrangement forms a marvelous pattern. The flavor is refreshingly acidic, yet at the same time delectably sweet, with a hint of melon, strawberry and gooseberry.

The fruit is of Chinese origin, but New Zealand is the main producer and responsible for its commercial success. Originally the fruit was called Chinese gooseberry but, to please the American market, the name was changed to kiwi. The success of the kiwifruit has been helped by the fact that it stores well—the fruit is picked unripe and allowed to open slowly. The fruit is also grown in the United States, Italy and Spain.

The **Hayward** is the best, and most common variety. Apart from the high vitamin C content, the pulp of the kiwifruit also contains an enzyme which tenderizes meat. The kiwifruit's vitamin C content is at least double that of a lemon.

Buying & Storing
Kiwifruit can be bought when firm and allowed to ripen at room temperature. Ripe fruit gives slightly. Ripe fruit can be stored in the refrigerator for a few days. Unripe fruit will ripen within 24 hours if stored in a plastic bag with a ripe banana.

Preparation & Cooking
The beautiful pulp has made the kiwifruit an ideal choice for garnishing. For the prettiest slices, peel, then cut the fruit crosswise in slices. Kiwi pulp is delicious eaten on its own— the fruit can be cut in half and the pulp scooped out.

Kiwifruit are used for Pavlova and they are perfect in fruit salads, offering a delicate flavor and stunning color. Kiwifruit slices are an ideal decoration for cheesecakes, mousses, flans and other cold desserts, while the pureed pulp can be used to make delicious mousses, ice creams, sorbets and jams.

Passion Fruit

A truly fragrant fruit, the best known type of passion fruit is the **Purple Granadilla** *(Passiflora edulis)*. The fruit is the size of an egg and has a thin purple skin which wrinkles and turns dark purplish-brown as it ripens. The orangish-yellow pulp inside is gloriously scented with a distinctive sweet-sour flavor. It has many small dark seeds which are not unpleasantly crunchy.

There is also the **Sweet Granadilla** *(Passiflora ligularis)* which is smooth-skinned and orange colored. The yellowish pulp is full of black seeds and is not as aromatic as the purple passion fruit.

The passion fruit is native to South America, but is now grown in hot areas all over the world. The Jesuit missionaries gave the plant its name—they used various parts of the flower to illustrate the Signs of the Passion. The fruit is rich in vitamin C.

Buying & Storing
A ripe purple passion fruit will have a wrinkled dark skin; it will keep refrigerated for a few days.

Preparation & Cooking
This perfumed fruit is perfectly delicious served with the top cut off so that you can scoop out the pulp with a spoon—add cream, if desired.

The pulp is often rubbed through a sieve, to remove the seeds, before use in recipes. The juice is sometimes available bottled; to make your own, heat the pulp with lemon or lime juice, then sieve.

The pulp adds an exotic scent to fruit salads, ices, fruit fools and jams and is particularly good spooned over ice cream or cream-filled meringue— it is a traditional topping for Pavlova. The juice makes a tangy, fragrant addition to cocktails, fruit punches and syrups.

Kiwifruit

*Purple Granadilla
(common Passion Fruit)*

Sweet Granadilla

Pineapple

The pineapple *(Ananas comosus)* must surely be one of the most popular tropical fruits. Pineapples resemble giant pine cones growing straight out of the ground with pointed plume-like leaves sprouting from the top. They vary in size enormously, depending on the variety, weighing from eight ounces to seven to nine pounds.

The outside of the pineapple consists of a series of scales varying in color from green to yellow through to orange. The juicy pulp inside can be pale, almost white, through to canary yellow, with a woody core down the center which is the remains of the flower stem. Between the skin and pulp there are cavities containing small stiff hairs which are called the eyes.

Pineapples have a very distinctive flavor—sweet, aromatic and acidic all at the same time.

Originally from Paraguay, the fruit was discovered by the Spanish and Portuguese conquistadores who named it *pina* (pine cone). It soon spread to other tropical countries and was even grown in England during the 17th century—in hot houses. As it took between two to three years for these pineapple plants to produce a fruit, it is not surprising that these early cultivated fruits were very expensive. By the 1870's steam ships were bringing pineapples to England from the West Indies and in 1900 when canning began, the fruit became more widely available.

Today pineapples are within most people's price range. The main exporters of pineapple are Africa, the West Indies, the Azores, Canary Islands, the United States, Mexico, Puerto Rico, with the best coming from Hawaii.

Pineapples should be left to ripen on the plant. The stem contains starch which is converted to sugar and rushes up into the fruit as it turns ripe. When this happens the pineapple doubles its sugar content overnight; if picked unripe, the sugar never reaches the fruit. Kiwifruit, papaya and pineapple contain an enzyme which breaks down protein.

Buying & Storing

Always buy ripe pineapples as they have the best flavor. Immature fruit will not ripen in a warm room but remain woody and tasteless, while overripe pineapple will taste fermented. To tell if the fruit is ripe for eating—smell it. It should have a strong pineapple aroma. The leaves should look fresh and you should be able to pull out a leaf easily from the center. Avoid any that look bruised. Refrigerated pineapples will keep for two to three days in a plastic bag.

Preparation & Cooking

Pineapples can be presented in so many ways. For simple slices, first twist off the leaves, then cut the fruit in slices. Cut away the skin and central core from each piece.

Alternatively remove the skin before slicing: hold the pineapple by the leaves, cut a slice from the bottom so that it stands upright, then cut away the skin in downward strips with a sharp knife. Cut out the hard eyes in diagonal strips, then slice or cut the fruit in wedges.

The pineapple skin, although inedible, makes a lovely natural container. Halve or quarter the fruit, cutting through the leaves so they remain attached. The pulp can be cut out, diced and replaced.

Or you can slice off the top with its leaves and, using a long knife, cut around the pulp leaving a solid wall. With a firm push, the pulp should come out in one piece. It can be sliced, returned to the shell and presented with the top on.

Pineapples are a most refreshing dessert fruit served by themselves or with the addition of a liqueur, such as kirsch or Grand Marnier. The fruit can be liquidized and made into a refreshing drink combined with alcohol, or made into sorbet and ice cream. Pineapple is delicious in sweet and savory salads, goes well with cheese, and is traditionally cooked with ham. It is the perfect companion for chicken, either cold or hot, and is often used in sweet and sour dishes. Gelatin will not set with fresh pineapple. Do not freeze pineapple.

Miniature Pineapple

Pineapple

Prickly Pear

Prickly Pear

The prickly pear, also known as the Barbary fig, Barbary pear, Indian fig and tuna fig is the fruit of the cactus plant *(Opuntia).* The name prickly pear is aptly descriptive for this oval fruit which is covered in tiny sharp spines. It is about three inches long and can vary in color from whitish-yellow to pinkish-orange, depending on the variety. The thin soft skin contains a deep-orange or red pulp full of hard brown seeds. Its taste has often been compared to that of a rather sweet cucumber.

Originally from the Americas, the prickly pear is also now found growing in India, North Africa and Europe, especially Sicily and southern Italy. The best varieties are the pink ones from Mexico and America. Eu-ropean varieties are white or yellow.

Buying & Storing
Avoid any that are overly soft. Prickly pears store well; unripe fruit will keep up to four weeks, ripe fruit for up to two weeks in the refrigerator.

Preparation & Cooking
Handle with care as the prickles are difficult to remove once they have become embedded in your skin. Use a knife and fork to peel them or slice in half and scoop out the pulp with a spoon. Eat as a dessert fruit; add to fruit salads; use sieved pulp as a sauce. Counteract the lack of acidity with some grated lemon or lime peel and juice.

Rhubarb

Rhubarb *(Rheum rhaponticum)* is not strictly a fruit but a vegetable—the leaf stem of plant; however it is treated as a fruit. It looks like a rather long pink stalk and has a tart acidic taste so that it must be cooked with sugar to be palatable. The leaves are poisonous owing to their high oxalic acid content.

There are generally two crops of rhubarb during the season. The first one, which is forced, produces thin pink tender stalks. The second crop, also called field or outdoor rhubarb, produces coarse thicker stalks with dark leaves and a more acidic flavor. For forcing, the root stocks are dug out and left on top of the earth, exposed to the weather, overnight. They are then transferred to a dark shed or barrel. The young plants grown quickly; rhubarb can grow at a rate of two inches a day.

Rhubarb has been grown for thousands of years for medicinal purposes in India, China, Mongolia and Siberia. It was first introduced to Britain from Siberia in the 16th century and was then grown as an ornamental plant. It was not until the 19th century that it was treated as a fruit, and was very popular during the Victorian era. Today rhubarb is cultivated in Britain, the northern states of America and north Europe. Of the many varieties developed through the centuries, over one hundred are still grown today. One of the best flavored varieties is **Champagne** or dresden rhubarb, a forced variety.

Buying & Storing
Always choose young pink rhubarb when possible. Forced rhubarb is less acidic than the older outdoor rhubarb. Avoid any stalks that are limp or split. It is an ideal fruit for freezing; blanch first.

Preparation & Cooking
Young pink rhubarb does not need to be peeled. Remove the leaves and cut off any discolored bits at the bottom end. Older outdoor rhubarb tends to be stringy and needs to be peeled. Cut in pieces, rinse and drain. It can then be stewed, steamed, baked or poached. Rhubarb is ideal for puddings, fruit fools and crisps; delicious made into a sauce or preserve and served with pork or deep-fried cheese. The older type of rhubarb is best for jams and chutneys whereas the forced rhubarb is good for canning and rhubarb wine. Flavor rhubarb with grated orange rind, rose water, ginger or cinnamon when cooking.

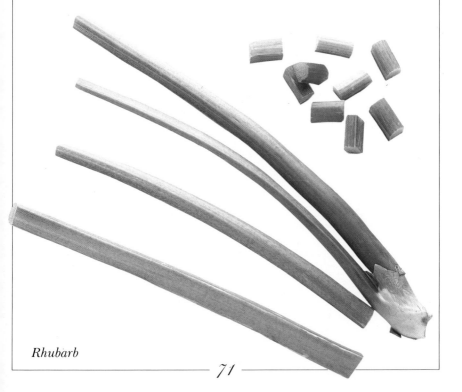

Rhubarb

Strawberry

The delicately-flavored strawberry *(Fragaria)* is perhaps the most popular of all the berries. The classic combination of strawberries and cream has long been one of the pleasures of the English summer, and today strawberries are still regarded as a luxury.

The heart-shaped fruits vary in size from the tiny wild varieties to the large, juicy cultivated strawberries; the flavor also varies according to variety and ripeness. An unusual and distinctive feature of all strawberies is that the seeds grow on the outside of the fruit, rather than in the middle.

For centuries, the only species known to Europe was the tiny, fine-flavored **Wild strawberry** *(Fragaria vesca)*. The **Alpine strawberry,** a slightly larger wild variety, became a popular type to cultivate, and the species known as **Hautboy** or Hautbois *(Fragaria moschata)*, was grown for its delicious musky flavor. These small strawberries eventually went out of fashion, mainly because they were impossible to improve in size. However, Alpine strawberries (both red and white colored) are still cultivated on a commercial basis, particularly in France, because of their exquisite flavor.

The large, succulent strawberries that are such a familiar sight today are American in origin. Most of them are hybrids bred from the wild **Scarlet strawberry** *(Fragaria virginiana)*. Today's popular varieties include the early season **Gorella,** a large glossy strawberry, often irregular in shape. The late season **Red Gauntlet** is another large strawberry, purplish-red in color with a slightly acidic taste.

Today strawberries are available year around—English ones, which are only available from June to July, are renowned for their fragrance and flavor, but varieties with better keeping qualities are now exported from countries such as Israel, Spain, the United States, Cyprus, Kenya and New Zealand.

Buying & Storing
Look for evenly colored, plump fruit, with fresh-looking leafy tops; avoid containers stained with juice, or covered in plastic wrap—the fruit may be squashed. Undoubtedly, strawberries that have ripened on the plant have the best flavor, so picking your own fruit is well worth the effort!

Strawberries are highly perishable and ideally should be eaten on the day of purchase. They will keep for up to two days, loosely covered, in the bottom of the refrigerator.

Strawberries tend to turn mushy if frozen whole, so the best way to freeze them is in puree form.

Preparation & Cooking
Traditionally, large strawberries are served as a dessert fuit, topped with whipped cream, but they also make a variety of superb-looking desserts.

To hull strawberries, twist off the leafy tops, removing the attached white stalks at the same time. Only wash the fruit if absolutely necessary—even then, quickly dip in cold water just before hulling.

Overripe strawberries are perfect for pureeing. To puree, crush the fruit with a spoon or mix in a blender, then press through a nylon sieve to remove the seeds if wished. Sweeten to taste with powdered sugar.

When serving strawberries and cream, try substituting half of the cream with sour cream, or serve with crème fraîche. The heart-shaped cheese molds, *coeur à la crèmes*, are traditionally served with fresh strawberries—a delectable combination. The flavor of strawberries can be enhanced by sprinkling the fruit with lemon or orange juice, rose water, wine or liqueur.

Whole fruits make stunning toppings to tarts, cheesecakes and meringue baskets, while sliced strawberries in whipped cream make a divine filling for choux pastry, shortcake or mille-feuilles.

Strawberry puree makes delectable fruit fools, ice cream and cold soufflés; small strawberries are best used to make delicious jam.

Gorella

Red Gauntlet

El Santa

Alpine Strawberry

Hapil

Raspberry

The delicate raspberry with its delicious flavor, is very popular.

Related to the blackberry, raspberries grow in the cooler regions of the northern hemisphere, wild or under cultivation. Most European varieties are from the species *Rubus idaeus.* Their origin is confused and they did not feature much in cooking until the 18th century. The American species *(Rubus strigosa)* yields many cultivated varieties.

The most common raspberries are crimson colored; there are also yellow, white and dark-purple ones. As raspberries thrive in damp woodland and a cool climate, Scotland provides an ideal environment; Scottish raspberries are reputedly the best in the world.

Buying & Storing
Selecting raspberries is tricky, as the fruit is extremely perishable. As with all berries, avoid stained containers. If possible, use on the day of purchase; otherwise refrigerate overnight.

Raspberries freeze very well; freeze in a single layer without covering, then pack into rigid containers. Defrost slowly in the refrigerator before serving. Freeze overripe raspberries in puree form.

Preparation & Cooking
Divine as a dessert fruit, topped with whipped cream, raspberries also have many culinary possibilities.

Raspberries need little preparation, since bought fruit will usually be trimmed of stalks and hulls. The delicate fruit does not respond well to washing, so wipe clean if necessary. To puree—ideal for bruised fruit—crush and press through a nylon sieve. Sweeten to taste with powdered sugar. Raspberries are often partnered with peaches—in Peach Melba for example. Melon and pineapple mixed with raspberries make a lovely fruit salad.

Raspberry puree makes refreshing sorbets, ice creams, jellies and sauces—add a touch of red currant juice to enhance flavor and color. Raspberries are particularly good used in a filling for hazelnut meringue, and in the classic Summer Pudding. They are also traditionally used to flavor vinegar.

Blackberry

Shiny, black, succulent-looking blackberries *(Robus ulmifolius)* are popular early-autumn fruits. The cultivated blackberries are larger and more juicy than the field type—a better choice for preserves and cooking. Mainly grown in the northern hemisphere, there are numerous cultivated varieties, which are difficult to tell apart.

Buying & Storing
Look for shiny, plump fruit. Avoid any containers that are badly stained with juice. If possible, use on the day of purchase; otherwise store in the refrigerator for no longer than a day.

Blackberries freeze well: freeze in a single layer without covering until firm, then pack; alternatively, layer with sugar.

Preparation & Cooking
Before using, wipe the berries clean and remove any stalks. Serve sprinkled with a little sugar, and topped with whipped cream, yogurt or cream cheese and sour cream

Blackberries are traditionally cooked with apples to make lovely pies or jams. Pureed and sieved blackberries are turned into fragrant fruit fools and sauces.

Loganberry

The loganberry *(Rubus loganobaccus)* is a cross between a raspberry and a blackberry, originating in California. It resembles a large raspberry, but has a sharper flavor, ideal for cooking. It is grown extensively in the United States. The **Tayberry** is a new variety with a delicate flavor. Buy and use loganberries as for raspberries.

Tayberry   *Raspberry*   *Loganberry*

American Raspberry   *Blackberry*   *Blueberry*

Dewberry

The dewberry *(Rubus caesius)* is similar to the blackberry but is bluish-grey in color and smaller in size, with a more delicate flavor. The berries are normally only seen in Britain and the United States.

Prepare and use in the same way as blackberries.

Cloudberry

The cloudberry *(Robus chamaemorus)* is similar in shape and taste to the blackberry, but is orange colored. Found mainly in northern Europe, it is used for jams and puddings.

Boysenberry

The boysenberry is a *Robus* hybrid, similar in taste to the loganberry. Large, juicy, wine-colored berries, boysenberries are particularly popular in the United States, especially for pies and jams.

Mulberry

The most common type is the black mulberry *(Morus nigra)*. When ripe, mulberries are purple-red and very juicy, with a sweet, yet refreshingly clean flavor.

Probably native to western Asia, the mulberry was known to the early Greeks and Romans. The berries have to be picked when they are completely ripe, which makes them difficult to grow commercially.

Mulberries are generally served raw with whipped cream, but they are equally delicious in pies, sorbets, ice creams and jams. They can also be made into wine, or added to cocktails. Prepare and use mulberries as for blackberries.

Cranberry

The bright red American cranberry *(Oxycoccus macrocarpus)*, with its refreshingly sharp flavor, is famous for the sauce it produces.

The cranberry originally grew wild in the bogs of North America and was gratefully adopted by the early settlers, who possibly recognized it as a large version of the European cranberry *(Oxycoccus palustris)*. With the increased popularity of the cranberry, Americans began to cultivate the fruit and it is now grown throughout North America.

The berries have a waxy skin which helps to keep them fresh for some time; they are referred to as bouncing berries because the good ones are said to be very bouncy.

Buying & Storing
Look for berries that are shiny-red, firm and plump. They will keep in the refrigerator for two to three weeks, or they can be frozen.

Preparation & Cooking
Cranberries are too sharp to be eaten raw, but their tart flavor lends itself to many cooked dishes. Wash the berries just before use. Cranberry skins burst quite violently on heating, so cook them covered. Add sugar after cooking otherwise the skins will toughen.

Cranberries feature in traditional American fare—in muffins, cakes, puddings, tarts, breads and the classic sauce that is served with Thanksgiving turkey. The sharp flavor of cranberries combines well with oranges—a cranberry and orange sauce is a perfect accompaniment to roast duck or venison. Cranberries also make excellent sorbets, soufflés and mixed compotes; the juice adds a good tang to drinks.

Blueberry

A small, round fruit, the blueberry has a thin, blue-black skin and a deliciously sweet, blue pulp. The American blueberry belongs to the *Vaccinium* family and is related to the wild European bilberry. It grows wild in the United States, thriving in bleak conditions.

The blueberry is extremely popular in American cooking, and today it is widely cultivated in the United States. Cultivated blueberries are now available in Britain.

Buying and Storing
Blueberries should be plump and have a good color. They will keep refrigerated for two to three weeks and can be frozen in a single layer uncovered and than packed into containers and covered.

Preparation & Cooking
Blueberries are wonderful served with sugar and cream or fromage frais. In American cooking, they are used to make the famous blueberry pie, as well as muffins, waffles, tarts and cobblers. Stewed blueberries make a delicious topping for ice cream and, mixed with apple, provide an excellent filling for crepes. Blueberries are also used for jams, pickles and wines.

Bilberry

Also known as blaebery and whortleberry (as a *myrtille* in France), the bilberry *(Vaccinium myrtillus)* is a juicy, blue-black berry that grows wild on the moors and hillsides of Europe and northern Asia. The bilberry looks like a smaller version of its relative, the blueberry, and is often mistaken for that fruit.

Because of the difficulties in picking the fruit, the bilberry is rather ignored today—a pity, as the refreshing flavor is quite delicious. The cultivated blueberry, which is easier to pick and a juicier fruit, overshadows the bilberry.

Served with whipped or sour cream, bilberries are a treat, but they can also be enjoyed in tarts, pies, jams and jellies. Prepare and use in the same way as blueberries.

Physalis Fruit

Cape Gooseberry

Chinese Lantern

The Physalis fruit has many species. Of the dozen which are cultivated, the most popular are the **cape gooseberry** or goldenberry *(Physalis peruviana);* the **ground cherry,** strawberry tomato or dwarf cape gooseberry *(Physalis pruinosa);* the **Chinese Lantern** plant or bladder cherry *(physalis alkengii)* and the **tomatillo,** jamberry or tomate verde *(Physalis ixocarpa).*

Cape Gooseberry: Like the rest of the physalis family this is characterized by the papery calyx surrounding its round small fruit. About the size of a cherry, the cape gooseberry turns a golden color when ripe. Its smooth skin encloses a soft pulp full of edible seeds, similar to a gooseberry but tasting more like a sharp, sweet, perfumed tomato. Although originally from South America, the cape gooseberry acquired its name when it became one of the most important cultivated fruits in the Cape of Good Hope in the 19th century.

Chinese Lantern: Perhaps the best known variety, this fruit has a red calyx which looks just like a lantern. It has an edible berry but, unlike the other members of the family, it is often just grown for its decorative appearance.

Ground Cherry: Originally from America, this fruit is similar to the cape gooseberry but with a smaller calyx and a sweeter taste.

Tomatillo: A large fruit the size of a tomato, completely filing out the calyx that surrounds it. The berry is similar to a small green tomato but rather sticky and bland tasting.

Buying & Storing
When choosing the smaller varieties of physalis, select those with straw-colored husks, indicating that they are ripe. If possible ask to peel back the husk—the berry inside should be smooth, firm, yielding slightly to the touch and a yellowish-orange color.

The berries will store for up to two weeks before completely ripening, but once ripened they should be eaten as soon as possible.

Preparation & Cooking
The papery husks should be peeled back and removed before the fruit is eaten. The smaller varieties of physalis can be eaten as dessert fruit, or stewed and made into jams, sauces and cakes. The most popular way to serve them is wrapped in vanilla fondant icing as petits fours. The larger tomatillo is best cooked; it is often used in Mexican dishes.

Red Currants

Black Currants

Currants, Black, Red & White

These all belong to the same family: *Ribes*. They are small round berries with a thin translucent skin surrounding a juicy, soft pulp, which contains a number of edible seeds. Those that are cultivated today came originally from northern Europe, North Africa and Siberia.

BLACK CURRANT

The black currant *(Ribes nigrum)* has a rather tart flavor, and is best cooked, made into sauces, or made in the famous French liqueur—Crème de Cassis. Black currants are especially rich in vitamin C.

RED CURRANT

The red currant *(Ribes rubrum)* and **white currant** (which is a variety of the same thing) tend to be less tart than black currants and can be eaten when ripe with lots of sugar.

Buying & Storing

Look for firm, clean fruit with a sheen; avoid any that look dusty or withered. Currants can be kept for up to ten days in the refrigerator, covered with plastic wrap. They are also excellent for freezing, either whole or as a puree.

Preparation & Cooking

Pick over the berries and discard any that are damaged. Then run a fork along the string (bunch) to remove them. All currants are excellent for stewing, compotes, pies, flans, jellies, jams, sauces and syrups. The famous Cumberland Sauce is made from red currant jelly and is a natural partner for roast lamb. Black currants are particularly good for syrup and the French liqueur made from black currants, Crème de Cassis, makes a refreshing aperitif, Kir, when mixed with white wine.

Gooseberry

The gooseberry *(Ribes grossularia)* belongs to the same family as the currant. It is a round berry which can be smooth or hairy, green, yellow or red, depending on the variety. There are basically two types of gooseberry—cooking and eating. The cooking variety tends to be smaller and tastes very sharp, whereas the eating variety are quite large and deliciously sweet tasting when eaten raw but tend to lose their flavor when cooked. Gooseberries are native to Europe and are cultivated in Britain, Germany, to a small degree in America and in northwest France.

Buying & Storing
When choosing gooseberries, avoid any that are dirty or bruised. The first small green berries have the best flavor for cooking. Gooseberries will keep for up to three weeks in the refrigerator if covered. Sweet dessert gooseberries do not freeze well, but stewed cooking gooseberries are ideal.

Preparation & Cooking
Remove stems from dessert gooseberries and cooking gooseberries that are to be stewed, or cooked in pies, puddings and flans. Do not bother to do this if they are to be sieved after they have been cooked.

Dessert gooseberries are delicous eaten by themselves. Cooking gooseberries are delicious made into compotes, fruit fools, pies, cobblers, jam, sauces and wine. They are particularly good with mackerel and can be made into a flavored vinegar.

Gooseberry

Red Gooseberry

Chilled Fruit Soup

6 ounces red currants
6 ounces black currants
6 ounces cranberries
1/2 cup sugar
1-1/2 cups medium-dry white wine
1 (2-inch) cinnamon stick
Finely grated peel and juice of 1 orange
1-1/4 cups water
1 tablespoon crème de cassis liqueur
2/3 cup dairy sour cream
TO DECORATE:
Black currant leaves, if desired

1. In a large saucepan, combine currants, cranberries, sugar, wine, cinnamon stick, orange peel and juice and water. Bring to a boil, lower heat and cook gently 15 minutes, until fruit is tender.

2. Discard cinnamon stick. Puree mixture in a blender or food processor, then press through a nylon sieve into a bowl to remove seeds. Cool, then chill 1-1/2 hours.

3. Stir crème de cassis into chilled soup. Pour into 4 to 6 chilled bowls. Carefully add a spoonful of sour cream to each bowl of soup. Use a skewer to feather sour cream in an attractive pattern. Serve immediately, decorated with black currant leaves, if desired.

Makes 4 to 6 servings.

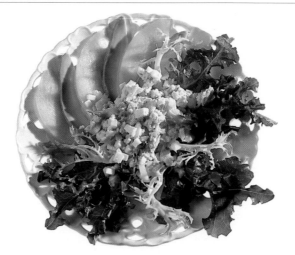

Crab Cocktail

8 ounces cooked crabmeat
1 celery heart, finely chopped
1 hard-cooked egg, finely chopped
2 tablespoons whipping cream
1 teaspoon tomato paste
8 drops hot-pepper sauce
1 Galia melon
1 large avocado
1 tablespoon lime juice
Salad leaves to garnish
LIME MAYONNAISE:
1 egg
1 tablespoon lime juice
1 teaspoon dry mustard
Salt and pepper to taste
1-1/4 cups olive oil

1. To make lime mayonnaise, in a blender or food processor, combine egg, lime juice, dry mustard, 1 teaspoon salt and a generous sprinkling of black pepper. While machine is running, gradually add olive oil in a thin steam through lid; blend until mayonnaise is thick and shiny.

2. In a large bowl, mix crabmeat, celery and hard-cooked egg. Stir in 3 to 4 tablespoons of mayonnaise, whipping cream, tomato paste, hot-pepper sauce and salt and pepper. Chill.

Cut melon in quarters, discarding seeds. Set aside.

3. Peel, pit and thinly slice avocado, then toss in lime juice to prevent discoloration. Cut melon in slices, same size as avocado slices. Cut away melon skin.

Spoon crab cocktail onto individual plates and arrange a fan of alternating melon and avocado slices on each. Garnish with salad leaves and serve immediately, accompanied by remaining mayonnaise.

Makes 6 servings.

Papaya & Prosciutto Starter

2 small papayas
4 ounces Prosciutto
4 small crisp lettuce leaves
Strip of pared lime peel
DRESSING:
1 papaya
1/2 cup crème fraîche
Juice of 1 lime
Few drops of hot-pepper sauce
Salt and pepper to taste
TO GARNISH:
Lime slices, if desired

1. To make dressing, cut papaya in quarters. Remove skin and seeds, then coarsely chop pulp. In a blender or food processor, blend chopped papaya, crème fraîche, lime juice, hot-pepper sauce and salt and pepper until smooth, then set aside.

2. Cut each small papaya in half, then cut each half in 3 slices, removing skin and seeds. Cut each piece of prosciutto in half lengthwise. Arrange 3 parallel papaya slices on each individual serving plate, then weave 3 strips of prosciutto through, forming a lattice.

3. Place a lettuce leaf on each serving plate and spoon dressing into center of each leaf. Cut lime peel in fine julienne strips and sprinkle over papaya. Garnish with lime slices, if desired. Serve immediately.

Makes 4 servings.

Fig, Ham & Mozzarella Salad

6 smoked ham slices
6 fresh figs
4 ounces mozzarella cheese, thinly sliced
8 ounces mixed salad leaves (such as radicchio, curly
endive or frisé, oak leaf, lamb's lettuce or mâche)
DRESSING:
1 garlic clove, crushed
1 teaspoon English mustard
1 teaspoon sugar
1/4 cup wine vinegar
1/4 cup plus 2 tablespoons olive oil
2 tablespoons hazelnut oil
Salt and pepper to taste

1. Preheat broiler. Divide ham among 6 individual gratin dishes or other shallow ovenproof dishes. Cut each fig in quarters lengthwise and place on top of ham. Cover with mozzarella cheese.

2. To make dressing, in a large salad bowl, mix garlic, mustard and sugar. Stir in vinegar, then gradually add olive oil. Add hazelnut oil, then salt and pepper. Add salad leaves to dressing and gently toss, ensuring all leaves are coated.

3. Place ovenproof dishes under grill about 3 minutes or until cheese has completely melted. Serve immediately with tossed salad leaves.

Makes 6 servings.

Tamarillo & Pasta Salad

1 pound pasta shells
1/3 cup olive oil
3 tamarillos
6 ounces goat's cheese, sliced or crumbled
DRESSING:
1/2 cup olive oil
1/2 cup red-wine vinegar
2 garlic cloves, crushed
1 green bell pepper, seeded, chopped
1 small onion, chopped
1 (4-oz.) can pimento, drained
3 tablespoons chopped parsley
3 tablespoons chopped basil
Salt and pepper to taste
TO GARNISH:
Sprigs of basil

1. In a large saucepan, cook pasta in boiling salt water 8 to 10 minutes or until just cooked *(al dente)*. Drain, rinse under tepid water and drain thoroughly. Transfer to a large bowl and pour olive oil over pasta, tossing pasta to ensure it is evenly coated. Cover with plastic wrap and refrigerate 30 minutes.
2. To make dressing, put all ingredients in a blender or food processor and process until smooth. Pour dressing over pasta and toss well.

Peel tamarillos and cut in thin slices.
3. Add tamarillos and goat's cheese to pasta and toss very gently. Transfer to individual serving plates and garnish with basil sprigs. Serve immediately.

Makes 6 servings.

Pear & Roquefort Quiches

1 cup all-purpose flour
Pinch of dry mustard
Salt and pepper to taste
1/4 cup margarine, diced
1/2 cup shredded Cheddar cheese (2 oz.)
1 to 2 tablespoons water
3 Comice pears
2 ounces Roquefort cheese
1/4 cup cream cheese (2 oz.), softened
2 eggs, beaten
1/2 cup whipping cream
1 tablespoon chopped tarragon
1 tablespoon butter, melted
DRESSING:
1 ounce Roquefort cheese
2 tablespoons sunflower oil
1 tablespoon tarragon vinegar

1. Sift flour, mustard and a pinch of salt into a bowl. Add margarine and cut in until mixture resembles bread crumbs; stir in Cheddar cheese. Mix in water to make a soft dough. Wrap in plastic wrap and chill 30 minutes. Preheat oven to 400F (205C). Roll out pastry thinly and line 4 greased deep 3-inch tartlet pans.

2. Peel, core and chop 1 pear. Beat Roquefort and cream cheese, then beat in eggs, whipping cream, tarragon and salt and pepper. Stir in chopped pear. Spoon into pastry cups. Peel and slice remaining pears. Arrange a few slices in a fan pattern on each tartlet. Brush with melted butter and bake in oven 20 minutes. Let stand a few minutes, then remove from pans.

3. To make dressing, in a bowl, cream Roquefort cheese until smooth, then beat in oil and vinegar. Season to taste with salt and pepper.

Serve tartlets warm or cold with a little dressing drizzled over.

Makes 4 servings.

Camembert with Rhubarb Preserve

8 individual portions of Camembert
1/2 cup all-purpose flour
2 eggs, beaten
1/2 cup toasted sesame seeds
Vegetable oil for deep-frying
Sprigs of herbs to garnish
PRESERVE:
1 pound rhubarb
2 tablespoons sunflower oil
1 large onion, sliced
1/3 cup cider vinegar
1/2 cup superfine sugar
1 (3-inch) cinnamon stick
3 whole cloves
1 (1-inch) piece fresh gingerroot, finely chopped

1. To make preserve, cut rhubarb in 2-inch slices. In a saucepan, heat sunflower oil, add onion and cook 5 minutes, until softened. Add rhubarb and cook, stirring frequently, 5 minutes. Pour vinegar over rhubarb and bring to a boil. Add sugar, cinnamon stick, cloves and gingerroot. Lower heat, cover pan and simmer 40 minutes, stirring occasionally, until all liquid is absorbed. Cool slightly, then discard cinnamon stick and cloves. Puree mixture in a blender or food processor. Transfer to a serving dish and cool.

2. Coat each portion of cheese with flour and then beaten egg. Roll in sesame seeds.

3. Heat oil in a deep skillet. When hot, deep-fry cheese, a few at a time, 30 seconds. Remove with a slotted spoon and drain on paper towels. Serve immediately, garnished with herbs and accompanied by rhubarb preserve.

Makes 4 servings.

Watercress & Apple Soufflé

2 bunches watercress, stalks removed
2 large cooking apples, peeled, thinly sliced
1/4 cup water
2/3 cup packed light-brown sugar
1 cup freshly grated Parmesan cheese (3 oz.)
4 egg yolks
1 tablespoon Dijon-style mustard
Salt and pepper to taste
1/4 cup butter
2 tablespoons all-purpose flour
2/3 cup half and half
5 egg whites

1. Butter 6 individual soufflé dishes. Chop watercress, reserving a few sprigs for garnish. In a small saucepan, place watercress, sliced apples, water and brown sugar. Cook over low heat, stirring occasionally, 15 minutes, or until apples are soft. Cool slightly, then puree in a blender or food processor. Transfer to a measuring cup; set aside.

2. Preheat oven to 450F (230C). Reserve 2 tablespoons of Parmesan cheese. In a bowl, mix egg yolks, remaining cheese, mustard and salt and pepper.

To make sauce, melt butter in a small saucepan over low heat. Remove from heat, stir in flour, then half and half. Cook 3 minutes, stirring constantly. Cool, then beat in egg yolk mixture and 1 cup of watercress mixture. Beat egg whites with a pinch of salt until stiff; fold into mixture.

3. Spoon into prepared soufflé dishes, sprinkle with remaining cheese and bake 5 minutes. Lower temperature to 400F (205C) and bake 10 minutes more. Serve immediately, accompanied by remaining watercress and apple puree in a separate bowl.

Makes 6 servings.

Mango & Shrimp Bundles

1 large mango, peeled, halved
12 ounces cooked peeled shrimp
2 green onions, finely chopped
6 large iceberg lettuce leaves
DRESSING:
1/2 cup mayonnaise
1 garlic clove, crushed
1 tablespoon mango chutney, sieved
2 teaspoons finely chopped cilantro
Salt and pepper to taste
TO GARNISH:
Lime slices
Sprigs of cilantro

1. From 1 half of mango, cut 6 thin slices; set aside for garnish. Cut remaining mango pulp in small cubes; place in a bowl with shrimp and green onions.

2. To make dressing, in a bowl, mix mayonnaise, garlic, chutney, cilantro and salt and pepper. Pour dressing over mango and shrimp and toss gently to ensure all ingredients are evenly coated.

3. Lay lettuce leaves on a work surface. Divide mango and shrimp mixture among them. Gently fold leaves over to form bundles, enclosing filling. Arrange bundles on individual plates, folded sides underneath.

Garnish with reserved mango slices, lime slices and cilantro sprigs to serve.

Makes 6 servings.

Shrimp with Lychees

1 pound lychees
3 tablespoons sunflower oil
1 bunch green onions, finely chopped
1 (2-inch) piece gingerroot, finely sliced
1-1/2 pounds uncooked peeled shrimp, thawed if frozen
8 ounces snow peas
1 tablespoon sesame oil
2 tablespoons saké or dry sherry
Salt and pepper to taste

1. Peel all but 8 lychees; set aside. Make 4 long cuts through skin and pulp of each unpeeled lychee from top to bottom. Peel back skin and pulp to form petals, leaving seed exposed to form center of flower; set aside.

2. Heat a wok or large skillet; add sunflower oil. When hot, add green onions and gingerroot and stir-fry 30 seconds. Add shrimp and stir-fry 2 minutes. Stir in snow peas and cook 1 minute. Add sesame oil and peeled lychees and cook 30 seconds. Add saké or sherry and salt and pepper.

3. Transfer to warmed individual serving plates. Garnish with lychee flowers and serve at once.

Makes 4 to 6 servings.

Curried Fish in Pineapple

2 small pineapples
1-1/2 pounds monkfish or swordfish, skinned
1 tablespoon butter
1 tablespoon vegetable oil
6 green onions, finely chopped
1 small chile, seeded, finely chopped
4 teaspoons garam masala or curry powder
1/4 teaspoon saffron threads
1 teaspoon ground cumin
1 tablespoon lime juice
1-1/4 cups whipping cream
1 cup slivered almonds (4 oz.), toasted
Salt and pepper to taste

1. Cut pineapples in half lengthwise through leaves. Cut out pineapple pulp, then cut in 1/2-inch cubes and set aside; reserve pineapple shells.
2. Cut fish in bite-size pieces. Melt butter and oil in a large skillet or wok over medium heat. Add green onions and chile and stir-fry 3 minutes. Stir in garam masala, saffron and cumin and cook 1 minute. Add fish and lime juice to pan and stir-fry 5 minutes. Pour in cream and bring to a boil. Lower heat and simmer 5 minutes, stirring frequently. Add pineapple cubes and 1/2 of aimonds. Season with salt and pepper. Cook 2 minutes.
3. Spoon curried mixture into pineapple halves. Sprinkle with remaining almonds and serve at once.

Makes 4 servings.

Note: Chile flowers make an attractive garnish for this dish. To make, slice chile lengthwise, leaving stem end intact. Place in a bowl of iced water until open.

Chicken & Pineapple Kabobs

3 skinned chicken breast fillets
1 large green bell pepper
1 small pineapple
6 bacon slices
3 bananas
MARINADE:
2 tablespoons soy sauce
1/3 cup pineapple juice
2 teaspoons finely chopped gingerroot
1 garlic clove, crushed
1 teaspoon dry mustard
2 tablespoons dry sherry
1 tablespoon olive oil
1 tablespoon lemon juice
TO GARNISH:
Salad leaves and chopped parsley

1. Cut each chicken fillet in 4 large chunks, then put into a bowl. Mix all marinade ingredients and pour over chicken. Refrigerate at least 2 hours.
2. Cut bell pepper in half, remove seeds and cut in 12 squares. Peel pineapple, cut in slices, then in chunks, discarding core.

Using scissors, cut each bacon slice in half crosswise. Cut each banana in 4 chunks. Wrap each banana chunk in a strip of bacon. Remove chicken from marinade, reserving marinade.
3. Preheat grill to medium. Thread prepared ingredients onto skewers in following order: pineapple, chicken, bacon-wrapped banana and bell pepper. Repeat twice more and finish with a pineapple chunk.

Brush with reserved marinade and grill about 20 minutes, until chicken is tender, turning and basting with marinade frequently. Serve immediately on a bed of salad leaves, sprinkled with chopped parsley.

Makes 4 servings.

Chicken with Cape Gooseberries

4 skinned chicken breast fillets
1 garlic clove, crushed
1 tablespoon finely chopped tarragon
Salt and pepper
1 tablespoon vegetable oil
1 tablespoon butter
6 shallots, finely chopped
SAUCE:
8 ounces cape gooseberries, peeled
3/4 cup dry vermouth
1 tablespoon sugar
2/3 cup dairy sour cream
TO GARNISH:
4 whole cape gooseberries
Sprigs of tarragon

1. To make sauce, put gooseberries in a small saucepan with vermouth and sugar. Cook over low heat, stirring occasionally, until sugar dissolves, then increase heat and bring to a boil. Cover and simmer 10 minutes, stirring occasionally. Remove from heat and strain gooseberries through a fine sieve into a bowl, pressing pulp through sieve with back of a wooden spoon; set aside.

2. Season chicken with garlic, tarragon, 1/4 teaspoon salt and a pinch of pepper; set aside. In a large skillet, heat oil and butter, add shallots and cook 2 minutes, stirring constantly.

Add chicken breasts and cook 6 minutes each side.

3. Pour strained gooseberry pulp into a saucepan. Add 1/4 cup of sour cream and cook over low heat 2 minutes, stirring; check seasoning.

Place chicken breasts on warmed individual serving plates and spoon over sauce. Top with remaining sour cream.

Peel back petals of skin from whole gooseberries to reveal fruit. Garnish chicken with gooseberry flowers and tarragon sprigs. Serve immediately.

Makes 4 servings.

Duck with Kumquat Sauce

1 (4-lb.) oven-ready duck
Salt and pepper to taste
1/2 cup superfine sugar
1/2 cup water
4 ounces kumquats
1/2 cup wine vinegar
Juice of 1 orange
1-1/4 cups chicken stock
1 tablespoon arrowroot blended with 1 tablespoon water
1 tablespoon orange-flavored liqueur
TO GARNISH:
Sprigs of parsley or cilantro

1. Preheat oven to 400F (205C). Prick duck skin all over with a fork; season with salt and pepper. Place on a rack in a roasting pan containing 1/4 cup plus 2 tablespoons water. Cook 1-3/4 to 2 hours or until tender.

Meanwhile, in a heavy-bottom saucepan over low heat, dissolve 2 tablespoons of sugar in water. Cut kumquats in slices and add to pan. Cover and simmer 15 minutes or until tender; set aside.

2. In another saucepan, dissolve remaining sugar in vinegar, then boil rapidly until reduced to a light caramel. Carefully add orange juice and stock and simmer 10 minutes.

Stir in blended arrowroot and cook over low heat, stirring until sauce is thickened and shiny. Stir in drained kumquats and liqueur; heat through gently.

3. Cut duck in half down breast bone, then cut each half in 2 portions. Arrange on a warmed serving dish and pour over sauce. Serve immediately, garnished with parsley or cilantro sprigs.

Makes 4 servings.

Note: If duck has giblets, use to make stock. If not, use chicken stock.

Tropical Beef Salad

3 cups white long-grain rice
1 pound boneless beef sirloin steak
2 garlic cloves, crushed
1 mango, peeled, diced
2 celery stalks, chopped
4 green onions, chopped
3 tablespoons raisins
2 bananas
3 tablespoons shredded coconut
DRESSING:
1 tablespoon prepared English-style mustard
2 tablespoons honey
2 tablespoons ketchup
1/4 cup cider vinegar
1/2 cup olive oil
Salt and pepper to taste

1. Cook rice in boiling salted water 10 to 15 minutes or until just tender. Drain, then rinse under tepid water; drain again. To make dressing, whisk all ingredients in a bowl. Pour over rice while still warm; mix gently.
2. Preheat grill to high. Spread steak with garlic and grill 2 minutes each side; steak should still be red in center. Cut steak in thin 1-inch-long strips.
3. Add steak strips, mango, celery, green onions and raisins to rice. Slice bananas diagonally and add to bowl; mix gently. Adjust seasoning if necessary. Transfer to individual serving plates. Sprinkle with coconut and serve at once.

Makes 6 to 8 servings.

Note: Green onion flowers make an appropriate garnish. To make, shred top lengthwise, leaving bottom intact. Place in iced water to open out.

Liver with Raspberries

12 ounces raspberries
2 tablespoons all-purpose flour
1 teaspoon dried leaf sage
Salt and pepper to taste
1 pound calves' liver, cut in thin strips
1/4 cup butter
1 tablespoon finely chopped sage leaves
1/4 cup raspberry vinegar
1/3 cup kirsch or framboise
2 teaspoons superfine sugar
Sage leaves to garnish

1. Set aside 12 raspberries for garnish. Puree remaining raspberries in a blender or food processor; strain and reserve.

Put flour in a flat dish and season with dried sage and salt and pepper. Coat liver strips with seasoned flour, shaking off excess.

2. Melt butter in a skillet. Add liver and fry 2 minutes, turning to brown on all sides. Add chopped sage and fry 1 minute. Transfer liver to a warmed plate with a slotted spoon and keep hot.

3. Skim off any excess fat from pan. Stir vinegar and kirsch or framboise into pan juices and cook 1 minute, stirring constantly. Add raspberry puree and simmer 1 minute. Stir in sugar and check seasoning.

Arrange liver on warmed individual plates and drizzle over raspberry sauce. Garnish with reserved raspberries and sage leaves. Serve at once.

Makes 4 servings.

Pork with Plums & Gin

1-1/2 pounds pork tenderloin
8 red plums
1/3 cup water
1 tablespoon superfine sugar
1 bay leaf
Salt and pepper to taste
1 tablespoon gin
MARINADE:
1 garlic clove, crushed
3 tablespoons olive oil
2 tablespoons gin
2 teaspoons lime juice
1 small onion, finely chopped
TO GARNISH:
1 or 2 plums, peeled, sliced
Sprigs of cilantro or parsley

1. Put pork into a shallow dish. Mix all marinade ingredients in a small bowl and pour over pork. Cover and refrigerate 4 hours, turning pork occasionally. Transfer pork to an oven-proof dish; reserve marinade.
2. Preheat oven to 350F (175C). Put plums into a bowl, cover with boiling water and let stand 1 minute. Peel, halve and remove pits. Add plums to reserved marinade. Stir in water and sugar. Add bay leaf and season with salt and pepper. Pour plum mixture over pork. Cover and bake in oven 40 minutes, until juices run clear when pork is pierced with a skewer.
3. Transfer pork to a warmed dish; keep hot. Skim off fat from cooking juices and discard bay leaf, then puree in a blender or food processor. Transfer plum puree to a small saucepan, add gin and boil 2 minutes; check seasoning.

Carve pork in slices and arrange on individual serving plates. Drizzle over plum sauce. Garnish with plum slices and cilantro or parsley sprigs. Serve at once.

Makes 4 to 6 servings.

Date & Lamb Pilaf

1 (2-lb.) lamb shoulder
3 tablespoons olive oil
1 large onion, finely chopped
3 garlic cloves, chopped
1 teaspoon ground cinnamon
1 teaspoon ground allspice
1/4 teaspoon ground ginger
5 cardamom pods, split open
12 ounces fresh dates
3 cups white long-grain rice
3 cups chicken stock
1 tablespoon grated orange peel
Pinch of saffron threads
Salt and pepper to taste
1/2 pomegranate
1/2 cup shelled pistachios

1. Cut lamb in 1-inch cubes. In a large flameproof casserole, heat olive oil, then add onion and garlic and fry 5 minutes or until softened. Stir in cinnamon, allspice, ginger and cardamom and fry, stirring constantly, 30 seconds.

Add lamb and cook 8 to 10 minutes, turning frequently to ensure lamb browns evenly.

2. Halve dates and remove pits. Reserve 1/2 of dates; chop remainder in small pieces and add to lamb. Add rice, stock, orange peel, saffron and salt and pepper; bring to a boil. Lower heat, cover and simmer 15 to 20 minutes or until liquid has been absorbed and rice is tender; stir occasionally during cooking.

3. Halve pomegranate and scoop out seeds, separating them; add seeds to casserole with pistachios and remaining dates. Cook 2 minutes to heat through. Check seasoning, adding more spice if necessary. Spoon onto a heated platter and serve at once.

Make 6 to 8 servings.

Blueberry Muffins

3 cups all-purpose flour
1 tablespoon baking powder
1/2 teaspoon salt
1/2 cup superfine sugar
2 eggs
2/3 cup milk
1/4 cup corn oil
8 ounces blueberries

1. Preheat oven to 400F (205C). Grease a deep 12-cup muffin pan. Sift flour, baking powder, salt and sugar into a large bowl; make a well in center.

2. In another bowl, lightly beat eggs; stir in milk and oil. Pour into well in flour mixture and, using a wire whisk, quickly mix flour into liquid ingredients; do not over mix—the mixture should be slightly lumpy. Quickly fold in blueberries.

3. Spoon mixture into greased muffin pan, filling cups 2/3 full. Bake in oven 20 to 25 minutes or until well risen and a fine skewer inserted into center of muffins comes out clean. Remove from oven and cool slightly in pan before turning out. Serve warm.

Makes 12 muffins.

Passion-Fruit Cake

2-1/2 cups all-purpose flour
1 teaspoon baking soda
2 teaspoons baking powder
1 cup packed light-brown sugar
1/2 cup walnuts, chopped
3 eggs, beaten
3/4 cup vegetable oil
3/4 cup grated carrot
2 passion fruit
3 bananas
Walnut halves to decorate
FROSTING:
1/4 cup plus 2 tablespoons margarine, softened
1/3 cup Neufchâtel cheese, softened
1 cup powdered sugar, sifted
Few drops of vanilla extract

1. Preheat oven to 350F (175C). Grease a deep 9-inch heart-shaped cake pan, then line with waxed paper.

Sift flour, baking soda and baking powder into a bowl. Stir in brown sugar, chopped nuts, eggs, oil and grated carrot.

Cut passion fruit in half and scoop out pulp; add to bowl. Mash bananas and add to mixture. Beat well.

2. Pour mixture into prepared pan. Bake in oven 40 to 50 minutes or until a skewer inserted into center of cake comes out clean. Turn out onto a wire rack to cool.

3. To make frosting, in a large bowl, beat margarine and Neufchâtel cheese. Add powdered sugar and vanilla; beat until light and creamy. Swirl frosting over top of cake and decorate with walnut halves.

Makes 1 (9-inch) cake.

Avocado Ice Cream

2 large avocados
2/3 cup packed light-brown sugar
3 cups whipping cream
1 teaspoon vanilla extract
3 ripe bananas, chopped
3 egg whites
TO DECORATE:
Sliced kiwifruit
Halved strawberries

1. Peel avocado and chop pulp in cubes. Puree in a blender or food processor with brown sugar, whipping cream, vanilla and bananas.

2. In a large mixing bowl, whisk egg whites until stiff. Gently fold avocado puree into egg whites. Transfer to a rigid plastic container, seal and freeze 1 hour or until mixture is frozen at edges. Turn into a bowl, beat thoroughly, then return to container and freeze 2 to 3 hours or until softly frozen through. Beat again, then freeze overnight.

3. Transfer to refrigerator 1 hour before serving. Serve scooped in balls and decorated with sliced kiwifruit and halved strawberries.

Makes 6 to 8 servings.

Lemon & Raspberry Bombe

Finely grated peel of 2 lemons
Juice of 3 lemons
2 eggs, separated
1 cup superfine sugar
1 cup whipping cream
6 ounces raspberries
Grated peel and juice of 1 orange
2 egg whites
TO DECORATE:
Raspberries
Shredded orange peel

1. In a small bowl, mix lemon peel and juice. In a large bowl, whisk 2 egg whites until stiff. Gradually whisk in 1/2 of sugar, then beat in egg yolks. In a separate bowl, whip 1/2 of cream until thick, then add lemon peel and juice and whisk until firm; fold into egg mixture. Pour into a rigid freezerproof container, cover and freeze until firm.

2. Put raspberries into a saucepan with remaining sugar and orange peel and juice; cook gently 5 minutes. Remove 1/2 of raspberries with a slotted spoon; set aside. Press remaining fruit and juice through a sieve into a bowl; cool. Whip remaining cream until thick and fold in whole raspberries and puree. Whisk remaining 2 egg whites until stiff and fold into mixture. Pour into a rigid freezer-proof container, cover and freeze until firm.

3. Chill a bombe mold, then line with lemon ice cream. Cover and freeze 30 minutes. Spoon raspberry ice cream into center of mold, level surface, cover and return to freezer until firm.

To turn out, rub mold with a cloth wrung out in hot water until bombe drops out. To serve, cut in wedges and decorate with raspberries and shredded orange peel.

Makes 6 to 8 servings.

Grapefruit & Mint Sorbet

3/4 cup superfine sugar
1/2 cup water
Juice of 2 grapefruit
Juice of 1 lime
1 tablespoon finely chopped mint leaves
2 egg whites
3 kiwifruit
TO DECORATE:
Sprigs of mint

1. In a saucepan, heat sugar and water gently until sugar is dissolved, then boil 5 minutes; cool. Strain grapefruit and lime juices into a bowl. Stir in cooled syrup and chopped mint. Turn into a freezerproof container, cover and freeze 2 to 3 hours, until half-frozen.
2. Whisk egg whites until stiff, then fold into half-frozen mixture. Return to freezer until just firm, then beat thoroughly and freeze until required.
3. Peel kiwifruit and puree in a blender or food processor; sieve to remove seeds, if desired.

To serve, cover plates with kiwi puree. Using 2 dessert spoons, shape ovals of sorbet and arrange three on each plate. Decorate with mint sprigs and serve immediately.

Makes 4 servings.

Sapote Sorbet in Baskets

SORBET:
About 3 pounds sapotes
1 cup superfine sugar
3/4 cup water
2 egg whites
1 tablespoon lemon juice
GINGER BASKETS:
3 egg whites
3/4 cup superfine sugar
1 teaspoon ground ginger
1/2 teaspoon ground cinnamon
Generous pinch of grated nutmeg
1 teaspoon finely grated gingerroot
1/4 cup plus 2 tablespoons unsalted butter, melted, cooled
TO DECORATE:
Sprigs of mint

1. To make sorbet, halve sapotes and scoop out 2 cups pulp. In a heavy saucepan, heat sugar and water over low heat until sugar is dissolved. Increase heat and simmer 5 minutes, then cool. Beat egg whites until stiff. Fold sapote pulp, egg whites and lemon juice into cooled syrup.

Turn into a rigid plastic container, seal and freeze 1 hour or until just set. Turn into a bowl and beat 2 minutes until mixture is light and fluffy. Return to container and freeze 2 to 3 hours or until solid.

2. To make ginger baskets, preheat oven to 400F (205C). Grease 2 large baking sheets. In a bowl, beat egg whites and sugar with a fork 30 seconds. Add remaining ingredients and mix thoroughly. Spread mixture in 6 to 8 (6-inch) circles on greased baking sheets, spacing well apart.

3. Bake in oven 8 to 10 minutes. Using a palette knife, carefully lift each circle and place inside a muffin cup or over bottom of a glass. Frill edges and cool, then carefully remove.

Transfer sorbet to refrigerator 30 minutes before serving. Scoop sorbet into ginger baskets and decorate with mint sprigs.

Makes 6 to 8 servings.

Cherries Jubilee

1/3 cup superfine sugar
Finely shredded peel of 1/2 orange
Juice of 1 orange
1-1/4 cups water
1 pound dark sweet cherries, pitted
1 (2-inch) cinnamon stick
1 tablespoon arrowroot
TO SERVE:
Vanilla ice cream
1/4 cup brandy
Sprigs of mint

1. Put sugar, orange peel, 1/2 of orange juice and water into a saucepan. Heat gently, stirring occasionally, until sugar has dissolved. Add cherries to pan and cook over low heat about 5 minutes, until they begin to soften. Using a slotted spoon, transfer cherries to a bowl; discard orange peel.

2. Add cinnamon stick to syrup in pan. Bring to a boil, then boil 3 minutes; discard cinnamon stick. Mix arrowroot with remaining orange juice and stir into syrup. Simmer, stir-ring constantly, until mixture thickens and becomes clear. Return cherries to pan and heat through.

3. Divide ice cream among 4 individual dishes. Heat brandy in a large metal ladle over an open flame, light and as soon as it flames, pour over cherries. When flames have died down, spoon cherries over ice cream and serve immediately, decorated with mint sprigs.

Makes 4 servings.

Oriental Fruit Salad

1 small watermelon
1/2 ogen melon
1/2 honeydew melon
1 pound rambutans
1 pound lychees
3 mangosteens
1 starfruit (carambola)
1/2 cup plum wine, saké or dry sherry

1. Sketch out a design for the side of the watermelon on a piece of paper; try to find a Chinese or Japanese symbol to copy. Using a non-toxic felt-tip pen, draw a design on skin of watermelon.

Cut off top 1/3 of watermelon, then using a melon baller, scoop out pulp in balls and place in a large bowl. Scoop out any remaining pulp with a large spoon.

2. Using a small sharp knife, carefully carve out design on skin of watermelon, making sure only dark-green skin is removed so that the lighter pith shows through.

3. Shape ogen and honeydew melon pulp in balls and add to bowl. Peel rambutans, lychees and mangosteens. Slice starfruit; add to melon balls. Add honey and plum wine, saké or sherry and mix gently. Spoon fruit into carved watermelon shell. Serve chilled.

Makes 6 to 8 servings.

Note: For a professional finish, leave a 1-inch strip of skin attached over watermelon to make a handle. Decorate with flowers.

If rambutans are unavailable, substitute lychees.

Nectarine Tart

1-1/2 cups all purpose flour
Pinch of salt
1/2 cup butter, diced
1 egg yolk
1 teaspoons superfine sugar
1 tablespoon lemon juice
1 tablespoon water
FILLING:
1/4 cup plus 2 tablespoons butter, softened
1/3 cup superfine sugar
2 eggs, beaten
3/4 cup ground almonds
1/4 cup plus 1 tablespoon apricot jam
2 nectarines
1 tablespoon lemon juice

1. Sift flour and salt into a bowl, then cut in butter. Make a well in center. In another bowl, beat egg yolk with sugar, lemon juice and water. Pour into well, then mix. Knead lightly to form a smooth dough. Wrap in plastic wrap and chill 30 minutes. Roll out pastry thinly and line an 8-inch loose-bottom flan pan.
2. Preheat oven to 375F (190C). To make filling, in a large bowl, beat butter and sugar until light and fluffy. Gradually beat in eggs, then stir in ground almonds.
 Spread 3 tablespoons of jam over bottom of pastry. Spread almond mixture over jam. Bake in oven 45 minutes, until top is light-golden. Cool slightly in pan, then transfer to a wire rack to cool completely.
3. Peel, pit and slice nectarines. Arrange in a spiral pattern on top of tart. In a small saucepan, gently warm remaining apricot jam with lemon juice. Sieve, then brush over nectarine slices. Serve tart cold, cut in wedges.

Makes 6 servings.

Mixed Berry Tartlets

1-1/2 cups all-purpose flour
Pinch of salt
1/3 cup superfine sugar
3 egg yolks
1/4 cup plus 3 tablespoons butter, softened
1 pound mixed berries (such as strawberries, raspberries,
red currants, black currants, blackberries)
1/4 cup red currant jelly
1 tablespoon water
CRÈME PATISSIÈRE:
2 egg yolks
1/4 cup superfine sugar
1 tablespoon all-purpose flour
1 tablespoon cornstarch
1-1/4 cups milk
1 tablespoon kirsch

1. Sift flour onto a cool flat surface and make a well in center. Add salt, sugar, egg yolks and butter to well. Using fingertips, work ingredients, gradually drawing in flour. Knead lightly to form a smooth dough. Wrap in plastic wrap and chill 1 hour.
2. Preheat oven to 400F (205C). Roll out pastry thinly and line 8 (3-inch) tartlet pans. Prick bottoms and chill 20 minutes. Bake in oven 10 minutes. Using fingertips, press puffed up pastry back in shape. Return to oven 5 to 10 minutes or until pastry is crisp and golden. Cool slightly in pans, then turn out.

To make crème patissière, in a bowl, mix egg yolks, sugar, flour and cornstarch. Mix in a little milk. Bring remaining milk to just below boiling point, then gradually add to egg mixture, stirring constantly. Pour back into pan; whisk over low heat until thickened. Cover with dampened waxed paper; let stand until cold.
3. Stir kirsch into cold crème patissière, spread in pastry cups, then arrange berries on top. Heat red currant jelly with water. Brush over fruit and let stand 2 hours to set before serving.

Makes 8 tartlets.

Baked Apple Bundles

1/4 cup mincemeat
1 tablespoon chopped pecans
1 tablespoon chopped angelica
1/4 cup calvados or brandy
4 large Cox's Orange Pippins or similar eating apples
8 sheets filo pastry
2 tablespoons butter, melted
2 tablespoons powdered sugar

1. Preheat oven to 350F (175C). Put mincemeat, pecans and angelica into a bowl. Stir in calvados or brandy and let stand 1 hour.

Grease a baking sheet. Core apples and place on a greased baking sheet. Spoon mincemeat mixture into apple cavities. Bake in oven 15 to 20 minutes. Remove and cool.

2. Lay 4 sheets of filo pastry on a flat surface. Brush liberally with melted butter, then cover each greased sheet of filo with another sheet of filo at a 45° angle.

3. Place an apple in center of each filo pile and gather up pastry around apple to make an 8-pointed bundle. Tie with string and place on baking sheet. Bake in oven 10 to 15 minutes. Remove string, dust with powdered sugar and tie with a ribbon. Serve immediately.

Makes 4 servings.

Orange Crepes with Pistachios

CREPES:
1 large egg, lightly beaten
2 tablespoons butter, melted
1-1/3 cups milk
1 cup all-purpose flour
Pinch of salt
1 tablespoon superfine sugar
Finely shredded peel of 1 orange
FILLING & SAUCE:
1 cup plain yogurt
2 teaspoons orange flower water
1/2 cup chopped pistachios
2 sweet oranges
1/4 cup honey
2 tablespoons Grand Marnier liqueur

1. To make filling, place yogurt in a bowl and stir in orange flower water. Add 1/2 of chopped pistachios. Chill.

To make sauce, peel and section orange. In a small saucepan, heat honey gently. Add orange sections and heat through gently 2 minutes. Stir in liqueur.

2. To make crepes, in a small bowl, mix egg, butter and milk. Sift flour and salt into a large bowl, then stir in sugar and orange peel. Make a well in center and add liquid mixture. Using a wire whisk, gradually mix liquid into flour to form a batter. Let stand 30 minutes.

Heat a 7-inch crepe pan over moderately high heat, then oil pan with a few drops of oil. Pour in about 2 tablespoons of batter and tilt pan to coat bottom evenly. Cook 1 to 2 minutes, until underside is golden-brown. Toss crepe and cook 20 seconds. Continue making crepes in this way, stacking them with waxed paper on a warmed plate as they are cooked; keep hot.

3. Just before serving, spoon a little filling onto each crepe and fold to form a triangle, enclosing filling. Arrange on individual plates. Pour sauce over crepes and sprinkle with remaining pistachios to serve.

Makes 4 to 6 servings.

Kiwi & Passion-Fruit Pavlova

MERINGUE:
4 egg whites
Pinch of salt
1 cup superfine sugar
1 teaspoon cornstarch
1 teaspoon white-wine vinegar
FILLING:
2 cups whipping cream
2 tablespoons superfine sugar
6 passion fruit
6 kiwifruit, peeled, sliced

1. Preheat oven to 275F (135C). Line a baking sheet with parchment paper. Draw a 9-inch circle on paper. To make meringue, beat egg whites with salt until stiff peaks form. Gradually beat in superfine sugar, then continue to beat 5 minutes. Fold in cornstarch and vinegar. Using a palette knife, spread meringue mixture evenly over circle on prepared baking sheet.

Bake in oven 10 minutes. Lower heat to 225F (105C) and cook 45 minutes more. Turn off heat and leave meringue in oven to cool slowly 1 hour. Remove from oven and carefully transfer to a plate.

2. To make filling, whip cream with sugar until thick. Cut passion fruit in half and scoop out pulp into a bowl. Fold pulp and 1/2 of kiwifruit slices into cream mixture.

3. Carefully spoon cream mixture over meringue, smoothing with a palette knife. Decorate top with remaining kiwi slices. Serve immediately cut in wedges.

Makes 6 to 8 servings.

Wild Strawberry Cheesecake

1-1/4 cups finely crushed graham crackers
1/2 cup finely chopped hazelnuts
1/4 cup plus 2 tablespoons butter, melted
1-1/2 cups cottage cheese
1/4 cup superfine sugar
3 eggs, separated
Finely grated peel and juice of 1 lemon
1 (.25-oz.) envelope unflavored gelatin (1 tablespoon)
1-1/4 cups whipping cream
12 ounces wild strawberries
3 tablespoons red currant jelly
2 teaspoons water

1. In a bowl, mix graham cracker crumbs and hazelnuts; stir in melted butter. Spoon into a deep 8-inch springform pan and chill until firm.
2. In a bowl, beat cottage cheese with sugar, egg yolks and lemon peel. Dissolve gelatin in lemon juice, then stir into cheese mixture. Whip cream until stiff peaks form; fold into mixture. Whisk egg whites until stiff, then fold in. Cover and chill 10 minutes, until beginning to set.
3. Spoon 1/2 of cheese mixture over

crust. Sprinkle 2/3 of strawberries evenly over cheese mixture. Cover with remaining cheese mixture. Chill 2 hours.

Remove cheesecake from pan and arrange remaining strawberries on top. Warm red currant jelly with water over low heat. Cool until thick enough to coat back of a spoon, then brush over top of cheesecake and strawberries. Let stand until set.

Makes 6 servings.

Exotic Fruit Brûlée

3 peaches
3 apricots
3 oriental persimmons
1 tablespoon plus 2 teaspoons finely chopped preserved
stem ginger
1 tablespoon rose water
1-1/4 cups whipping cream
1 tablespoon powdered sugar
1/3 cup superfine sugar

1. Peel peaches and apricots. Discard pits; slice peaches and apricots thinly and place in a bowl. Peel persimmons and slice thinly; add to bowl with chopped ginger. Pour over rose water and mix gently.

2. In a separate bowl, whisk cream with powdered sugar until stiff; gently fold into fruit mixture. Spoon into 6 ovenproof ramekin dishes. Cover with plastic wrap and chill 2 hours.

3. Preheat broiler. Sprinkle superfine sugar over top of each dish. Place ramekins on a broiler rack under hot broiler 2 to 3 minutes or until sugar has caramelized. Cool and serve cold.

Makes 6 servings.

Note: If oriental persimmons are unobtainable, use a ripe mango instead.

Strawberries Romanoff

1 quart strawberries
3 tablespoons powdered sugar
Grated peel and juice of 1 orange
1-1/4 cups whipping cream
1/2 cup Cointreau or other orange-flavored liqueur
2 tablespoons brandy
TO DECORATE:
6 to 12 strawberries
Shredded orange peel

1. Put strawberries in a large bowl and sprinkle with 2 tablespoons of powdered sugar. Add orange peel and juice and liqueur. Mix gently. Cover bowl with plastic wrap and refrigerate 30 minutes.
2. In another bowl, whisk whipping cream, brandy and remaining powdered sugar until fairly stiff. Cover with plastic wrap and refrigerate 30 minutes.
3. Spoon strawberries with juice into 6 individual glass serving dishes. Top with brandy-flavored cream and decorate with strawberries and shredded orange peel. Serve immediately.

Makes 6 servings.

Note: Crisp thin shortbreads or langue de chat cookies are ideal served with this dessert. Serve any remaining brandy-flavored cream in a separate bowl.

Citrus Mousse

2 eggs
2 egg yolks
1/2 cup superfine sugar
Finely grated peel and juice of 1 lemon
Finely grated peel and juice of 1 lime
Finely grated peel and juice of 1 large orange
2 tablespoons Cointreau or other orange-flavored liqueur
2 cups whipping cream
1 (.25-oz.) envelope unflavored gelatin (1 tablespoon)
3 tablespoons water
TO DECORATE:
Shredded lemon, lime and orange peel

1. Put eggs, egg yolks, sugar and grated peel in a bowl set over a pan of gently simmering water. Whisk until thick. Remove from heat and continue whisking until cool. Strain fruit juices into a measuring cup to make 3/4 cup; add extra orange juice if necessary. Gradually whisk juice into egg mixture, then whisk in liqueur. Whip 1-1/4 cups cream until it forms soft peaks; fold into mousse.
2. Dissolve gelatin in water, then fold into mousse mixture. Set bowl over iced water and stir until beginning to set, then turn into a glass serving dish. Chill 2 hours until set.
3. Whip remaining cream until stiff enough to pipe. Decorate mousse with piped cream rosettes and shredded lemon, lime and orange peel. Serve as soon as possible.

Makes 4 to 6 servings.

Pear Mousse & Chocolate Sauce

1/2 cup medium-dry white wine
1/3 cup superfine sugar
2 pared lemon peel strips
3 Bartlett or Conference pears
3/4 cup fromage frais or ricotta cheese
2 eggs, separated
1-1/4 cups whipping cream
2 tablespoons Poire William liqueur
2 (.25-oz.) envelopes unflavored gelatin (2 tablespoons)
3 tablespoons water
4 (1-oz.) squares semisweet chocolate
12 rose leaves
2 to 3 tablespoons strong black coffee

1. Put wine, 2 tablespoons of sugar and lemon peel into a saucepan; stir over low heat until sugar is dissolved. Peel, core and slice pears; add to syrup and poach gently 15 minutes. Cool and discard lemon peel. Strain mixture through a sieve, pressing pear pulp through back of a wooden spoon.
2. Drain fromage frais, then beat in egg yolks, and remaining sugar. Beat in 3/4 cup of cream, liqueur and pear puree. Dissolve gelatin in water. Stir a little pear mixture into dissolved gelatin, then stir gelatin into rest of pear mixture. Whisk egg whites until stiff, then fold into pear mixture. Divide among 6 ramekins and chill 6 hours.
3. Melt chocolate in a small bowl set over a pan of hot water. Brush underside of each rose leaf with melted chocolate; place on waxed paper in a cool place; reserve remaining chocolate. When chocolate leaves have set, carefully peel away rose leaves.

Warm reserved chocolate, if necessary, until melted, then stir in coffee and remaining cream to make a thin sauce; cool.

Turn mousses out on to individual plates, top with chocolate leaves and pour sauce around.

Makes 6 servings.

Guava Jelly

2 pounds guavas
2-1/2 cups water
Juice of 2 lemons
Sugar

1. Peel and slice guavas, discarding seeds. Place guavas, water and lemon juice in a large saucepan. Bring to a boil, then simmer 1 hour until tender. Hang a scalded jelly bag above a large bowl. Pour fruit into bag and drain at least 1 hour; do not squeeze bag.
2. Measure strained juice and place in cleaned pan. Add 1 pound sugar to every 2-1/2 cups strained juice. Bring to boiling point, then boil rapidly, about 20 minutes. To test, dip a metal spoon in mixture. When jelly falls off spoon in sheets, not drops, it's done.
3. Remove jelly from heat and let stand 15 minutes, until foam rises to surface; skim off with a slotted spoon. Meanwhile, sterilize 3 to 4 (1/2-pint) jars and lids and keep warm. Pour jelly into sterilized jars. Cover with melted wax and attach lids. Cool, label and store in a cool, dark place.

Makes 3 to 4 (1/2-pint) jars.

Rumtopf with Nutmeg Cream

5 pounds mixed soft fruit (such as strawberries, raspberries, peaches, plums, nectarines)
2-1/2 pounds superfine sugar
1 (750 ml.) bottle dark rum
NUTMEG CREAM:
1-1/4 cups whipping cream
1 egg white
3 tablespoons powdered sugar
Few drops of vanilla extract
1 teaspoon freshly grated nutmeg

1. Prepare all fruits, hulling, pitting and slicing as necessary. Put 1 pound of fruit in a 1-gallon preserve jar with an airtight lid. Sprinkle with 1 cup of superfine sugar and let stand 30 minutes. Pour over rum to cover fruit by about 1 inch.

2. Repeat this layering process with remaining fruit, sugar and rum to fill jar. Seal and store in a dark place about 4 to 5 months. Stir every few weeks.

3. To make nutmeg cream, in a bowl, whisk cream until fairly stiff. In another bowl, whisk egg white until stiff. Fold egg white, powdered sugar, vanilla and nutmeg into whipped cream. Transfer to a serving dish. Cover with plastic wrap and chill 1 hour. Serve rumtopf with nutmeg cream.

Makes 1 quart of rumtopf; makes 6 to 8 servings nutmeg cream.

Babaco Daiquiris

1 (8-oz.) babaco
1/2 cup white rum
2 tablespoons superfine sugar
1/4 cup lime juice
2 cups crushed ice
PLANTAIN CHIPS:
3 green plantains
Vegetable oil for deep frying
Salt to taste
1/4 cup toasted sesame seeds
TO DECORATE:
4 babaco or starfruit (carambola) slices
Lime peel twists

1. To make plantain chips, peel plantains and cut in thin slices. Heat oil in a deep-fryer until very hot. Add plantain slices, a few at a time, and fry 2 to 3 minutes until crisp and golden. Remove with a slotted spoon and drain on paper towels. Sprinkle with salt and sesame seeds. Cool.
2. Chill 4 cocktail glasses. Peel and chop babaco. Put babaco, rum, sugar, lime juice and crushed ice into a blender or food processor.
3. Blend mixture at high speed 30 seconds. Pour into chilled cocktail glasses and decorate with babaco or starfruit slices and lime peel twists. Serve immediately with plantain chips.

Makes 4 cocktails.

Papaya Cocktail

1 medium-size papaya
2/3 cup cream of coconut
2/3 cup freshly squeezed orange juice
Juice of 1/2 lime
1 cup crushed ice
TO DECORATE:
4 lime slices
4 orange slices
4 sprigs of mint

1. Chill 4 cocktail glasses. Peel papaya and chop pulp, discarding seeds.
2. Put chopped papaya, cream of coconut, orange and lime juices and crushed ice into a blender or food processor. Blend at high speed 1 minute or until mixture is smooth.
3. Pour into chilled cocktail glasses and decorate with lime and orange slices and mint. Serve immediately.

Makes 4 cocktails.

Variation
Watermelon & Gin Cocktail: Replace papaya, cream of coconut and orange and lime juices with 3/4 cup seeded chopped watermelon, 2/3 cup gin, 2 tablespoons superfine sugar and 1 tablespoon lemon juice. Blend, as above, with crushed ice. Decorate rim of glasses with triangles of watermelon and nasturtium flowers, if desired.

— INDEX —